CURIOUS CASES: TRUE CRIME FOR KIDS

HIJINKS, HEISTS, MYSTERIES, AND MORE

REBECCA VALLEY

BLOOM BOOKS
FOR YOUNG READERS

Published by:
Bloom Books for Young Readers,
an imprint of Ulysses Press
PO Box 3440
Berkeley, CA 94703
www.ulyssespress.com

ISBN: 978-1-64604-349-1 paperback
ISBN: 978-1-64604-384-2 hardback
ISBN: 978-1-64604-369-9 ebook
Library of Congress Control Number: 2022932321

Printed in the United States by Versa Press
10 9 8 7 6 5 4 3 2 1

Acquisitions editor: Casie Vogel
Managing editor: Claire Chun
Project editor: Renee Rutledge
Editor: Scott Calamar
Front cover design: Rebecca Lown
Artwork: shutterstock.com
Production: Winnie Liu

IMPORTANT NOTE TO READERS: Although the author and publisher have made every effort to ensure that the information in this book was correct at press time, the author and publisher do not assume and hereby disclaim any liability to any party for any loss, damage, or disruption caused by errors or omissions, whether such errors or omissions result from negligence, accident, or any other cause.

CONTENTS

INTRODUCTION: WHAT DETECTIVES DO

This is a book about crime, so I want to begin with a confession. I am not a detective, in the proper sense of the word. I don't spend my days chasing criminals down dark alleys or dusting doorknobs for fingerprints. I started my journey into the world of mysteries just like you are now: by reading.

Over the years, I've had dozens of jobs. I've been a librarian and a teacher. I've mopped floors in a children's museum and shuffled papers from one filing cabinet to another in many boring offices. Once, while working at a summer camp in Vermont, I was tasked with steering a biplane full of middle schoolers thousands of feet above the Green Mountains. But while I was doing all those jobs, I was also doing what I loved best: reading and writing. And it was through that reading and writing that I learned something important. I learned that anyone can solve a mystery if they put their mind to it.

Despite what you see on TV, most detectives will tell you that crimes are rarely solved by brute force. Being a detective isn't about breaking down doors or chasing speeding cars. Crimes are solved with observation, critical thinking, and, most important of all, perseverance. And those are skills you can hone no matter how strong or fast or brave you are.

Sometimes, a detective is a person with a badge. But often, detectives are hiding in plain sight. Detectives can be writers who share stories about people that time, and law enforcement, have forgotten. They can be genealogists who identify victims and suspects by studying the human genome. They can be lawyers who advocate for people in a courtroom, and bone experts like Medicolegal Death Investigator Kristen Smith, who use their medical knowledge to find out how and why a person has died. They can be social workers who help crime victims find justice, and historians who dive into dusty filing archives to solve real mysteries hiding deep in the past. They can be the family members, friends, and neighbors of victims who gather case notes to try to find answers for someone they love. They can be scientists who bring previously unknown truths to light. They can be librarians, those expert sleuths who can find virtually any answer in a book.

What I'm trying to say is: Even you can be a detective. You don't need fancy skills. You can be a detective by reading carefully, evaluating evidence, and asking tough questions. Because the truth is, you are a detective every time you get curious. You are a detective when you start to ponder all the things in the world that we don't understand yet—even if you aren't sure you'll ever find an answer. You are a detective every time you say to yourself: "This is a story that means something to me, and I am going to get to the bottom of it."

In this book, some of the characters are detectives, and some are criminals. Some are tricksters, and others get tricked. Some are victims, and some are heroes. But often, everyone in the story is a little bit of all these things. As you'll soon discover, even the most notorious criminals have a good side, and even the best detectives sometimes get it wrong. While you read through these fifteen stories, remember to keep your eyes—and your mind—open. Because no mystery is as simple as it seems on the surface.

Do you have a mystery you'd like to solve?
Write to me about it at: morecuriouscases@gmail.com.

A TIMELINE OF FORENSIC SCIENCE

Forensic scientists use science to process evidence and help detectives solve crimes. Though some methods, like DNA analysis, have only been around for the past few decades, forensic science dates all the way back to the Roman Empire, when the first doctor performed an autopsy to find out how Emperor Julius Caesar died.

Some stories in this book are from the mid-1800s, when we had few scientific tools to solve crimes. Others took place just a few years ago. You can use this timeline to help you keep track of what scientific methods were available when each of these stories took place, and to learn more about how forensic science has changed over the hundreds of years we've been using it to solve crimes.

44 BC: The first autopsy (an investigation to determine the cause of someone's death) was performed by Antistius, a Roman doctor. He was investigating the death of Emperor Julius Caesar.

AROUND 1000 AD: Quintilian, a Roman lawyer, used basic forensics to stop his client from being accused of a crime. He proved that a bloody palm print was meant to frame someone.

1248: A Chinese book called *Hsi Duan Yu* is the first book ever to share how medical knowledge can be used to solve crimes.

1773: A Swedish chemist named Carl Wilhelm Scheele developed a test to detect arsenic, a deadly poison, in bodies.

1835: A Scotland Yard detective named Henry Goddard became the first person ever to solve a crime by matching a bullet to a specific murder weapon.

1870s: Photography becomes a commonly used technique to document criminals and crime scenes. The idea of the "mug shot" becomes popular at this time when photographers take photos of prison inmates. Photos are also used to document evidence at crime scenes.

1880: Sir Francis Galton developed the first fingerprint-matching techniques, which made it possible for police to use fingerprints at the scene to catch criminals. He published a book on the technique in 1892.

1880s & 1890s: French forensic scientist Dr. Edmond Locard becomes famous for his theory that "every contact leaves a trace," meaning that every criminal will leave something behind at the scene of the crime. He later became known as the "Sherlock Holmes of Lyon."

1900: Karl Landsteiner won a Nobel Prize for detecting that there are many different types of blood (for example, type A and type O). His discovery was used in forensic science to match suspects to crime scenes.

1901: Both English and American police start using fingerprints to identify criminals.

1902: Professor R. A. Reiss created the first forensic science classes at the University of Lausanne, Switzerland. He would become famous for his work on forensic photography. The department he created is still operational and is now called the Institute of Police Science at the University of Lausanne.

1908: The Federal Bureau of Investigation (FBI) is created by President Theodore Roosevelt.

1923: It became illegal to use polygraph test results in court as evidence, because experts discovered they are often inaccurate.

1924: The first crime lab in the United States was created by the Los Angeles Police Department in California.

1932: The first FBI crime laboratory was created.

1950: A Swiss forensic scientist named Max Frei-Sulzer created the tape-lift method of collecting small pieces of evidence, sometimes called "trace evidence."

1953: Paul L. Kirk published *Crime Investigation*, which was the first book that shared techniques and theories of forensic science, and how they can be used to solve crimes.

1977: The FBI introduced their new Automated Fingerprint Identification System, also called AFIS, which could scan and compare fingerprints using a computer.

1984: Sir Alec Jeffreys created the first-ever DNA profiling test.

1986: Sir Alec Jeffreys used his DNA profiling technology for the first time to solve a criminal case in England. During the investigation, DNA was used to prove that a suspect was, in fact, innocent.

1987: DNA profiling is used for the first time in a United States court.

1991: Scientists develop automatic facial recognition technology, which can analyze and identify faces from a photo or video.

2015: Scientists begin to study whether they can use fingerprint analysis to not only tell who was at the scene of the crime, but also how long the fingerprint has been there. This technology will help police narrow down a timeline of events after a crime, and potentially clear suspects who may have been present at the scene long before a crime was committed.

2018: Investigators and amateur sleuths start using ancestry data (also called genetic genealogy) on websites like Ancestry .com to identify both victims and suspects in criminal cases. If there is no DNA match in the police system, researchers can use genetic genealogy to find relatives of victims or suspects and narrow down the search.

PART ONE

CURIOUS CASES

CHAPTER ONE

THE DISAPPEARANCE OF MASTERPIECE THE POODLE

In New York City in the 1950s, poodles were everywhere. Walk down a street on the Upper East Side of Manhattan, and you might see a dozen poodles of all shapes and sizes—toy poodles, miniature poodles, standard poodles, all with custom haircuts and outfits. Poodles were the ultimate fashion accessory for elite New Yorkers. You could dress them up to match your favorite sweater or take them to the office in a tiny suit coat.

One newspaper wrote at the time: "When a girl makes the big time, she traditionally acquires three things: minks, gems, and a poodle."[1]

But it wasn't always like this. One dog, in particular, was responsible for bringing poodles into the spotlight. This canine was featured on TV and awarded gold medals by foreign governments. He sat on a velvet throne and led parades down Fifth Avenue. At one point, the newspapers called him the most valuable dog in the world.

His name was Masterpiece.

COUNT PULASKI AND HIS POODLES

Alexis Pulaski, known as "Count" Pulaski by his friends, wasn't always a poodle man. He arrived in New York in 1926, one of many "Russian Whites" who fought the communists during the Russian Civil War. He was part of a wave of Russian exiles who came to the United States after communists took over the Russian government.[2]

Even though he wasn't actually a count (his immigration paperwork reveals that "Count" may have been his middle name, but it definitely wasn't an official title), Pulaski was tall, elegant, and well dressed. Rich and fashionable New Yorkers liked him because of his good looks, accent, and European manners. Soon, he had charmed his way into every cocktail party in the city.

Back in Russia, Pulaski bred Doberman Pinschers. When he got to New York, he continued breeding and grooming dogs and started a small photography business. Business was good, though never booming. But that would change one weekend in 1939, when Pulaski's whole world was transformed. While babysitting his friend Gilbert Kahn's poodles, he fell madly in love—not with a person, but with a dog. Pulaski gave up his Dobermans, bought a poodle, and never looked back.[3]

THE RISE OF POODLES, INC.

Pulaski opened Poodles, Inc. in 1945 using money he acquired from a few rich, poodle-loving friends. The shop was located at 51 West Fifty-Second Street and would soon become the hub for poodle culture in Manhattan.[4]

Poodles, Inc. was a one-stop shop for all things poodle. It was a dog kennel (really, a resort), where you could leave your pups for a weekend trip. It was also a breeder, groomer, and supply store for high-end merchandise that you couldn't get anywhere else. Brynn White, the archivist for the American Kennel Club, calls it a poodle "haberdashery,"[5] because it was as extravagant as Manhattan's finest boutiques. Poodles, Inc. offered haircuts, clothing, accessories—even hair-dying services and dog furniture. But it wasn't a store for just any dog. This shop only catered to poodles and their owners. Because of that, Poodles, Inc. was soon transformed from a simple dog kennel into one of the most elite social clubs in the city.

As part of his work at Poodles, Inc., Pulaski got back into dog breeding. He bred dozens of litters of puppies—but on August 4, 1946, a special dog arrived. He was a tiny, gray toy poodle. He only weighed a few pounds. Pulaski was immediately drawn to him. He claimed that the puppy had "aristocratic airs,"[6] as well as uncommonly clean habits.[7] He knew from the beginning that this dog was more than just your average poodle.

Pulaski called his new friend "Pulaski's Masterpiece."

THE MOST VALUABLE DOG IN THE WORLD

From the beginning, Pulaski had plans to show Masterpiece at the Westminster Kennel Club Dog Show, one of the most well-known dog shows in the world. But the puppy got off to a rough start. In 1947, when he was only one year old, he caught distemper, a highly contagious virus. He nearly died, and Pulaski had to send him to a kennel in New Jersey to recover.

But that was not the last the world would see of Masterpiece. The following year, he came back with a bang and became the first toy dog ever to receive the Westminster trifecta: Masterpiece was awarded the championship prize and given first place in the utility and obedience titles. After making dog show history, Masterpiece and Pulaski began to tour around the United States, competing in shows from St. Louis to Los Angeles.[8]

The more awards that Masterpiece racked up, the more of a celebrity he became. Pulaski had special clothes made for his champion, including a tiny raincoat and pajamas with a matching bathrobe. Masterpiece had his own press agent, a bodyguard, and a private stylist. He even had his own perfume—a custom blend called "Kennel No. 9." Pulaski brought in a lion tamer from the Bronx Zoo to teach Masterpiece circus tricks, which the dog would perform at parties and in the lobby of Poodles, Inc. Unfortunately, the lion tamer died just before he could teach Masterpiece how to walk a tightrope.[9] The dog was known for one trick in particular—when Pulaski asked him, "Masterpiece, are you a communist?" the dog would shake his head "no." If Masterpiece was having an off day, Pulaski would pay someone to feed the dog by hand.[10]

At the height of his fame, Masterpiece even starred in his own parade. He led a group of more than seventy poodle friends up Fifth Avenue to a department store called Milgrim. At the Milgrim fashion shop, Masterpiece was put in a window display, seated on a green velvet throne. He was surrounded by Poodles, Inc. puppies.[11]

Masterpiece wasn't only popular in the United States. He was named an official goodwill ambassador to Cuba. In Haiti, he received a gold medal from the government. Masterpiece was an international phenomenon—and arguably, the most famous poodle in the world.

As Masterpiece's fame grew, so did his value. At one point, the Pakistani prince Aly Khan wanted to buy the dog from Pulaski. He offered him $25,000, the equivalent of almost $250,000 today. Pulaski, of course, rejected his offer. At the time, Masterpiece was making $11,000 per year (more than $100,000 in today's money) as a stud dog and model. According to Pulaski, Masterpiece refused to mate with a female dog for less than $500. His puppies could sell for as much as $2,500 apiece. Masterpiece made so much money, he had to have his own bank account.[12]

As part of his status as a celebrity, Masterpiece was often asked to go on talk shows. His last public appearance was on *The Dave Garroway Show* in 1953. He was asked to model new outfits for Easter. Just a few weeks later, in May, Pulaski went to the basement of Poodles, Inc. to chat with some staff members. When he came back up to the showroom, he whistled for Masterpiece, but the dog didn't come. The staff searched everywhere for their poster dog, but they could not find him.

It appeared, as Pulaski said, that "the greatest dog in the world had disappeared off the face of the earth."[13]

THE WOMAN IN RED

Pulaski immediately notified the police, and they sounded an alarm across thirteen states. Masterpiece's photo appeared on more than 3,500 flyers, which were printed and distributed by one of his corporate sponsors. Poodles, Inc. guaranteed a reward for Masterpiece's safe return, and Pulaski even went on national television to offer one of Masterpiece's puppies, a little gray poodle named Johnny, in exchange for his prized dog.

But no matter what Pulaski did, no one seemed to have information about the whereabouts of Masterpiece.

There were a few theories about what may have happened to the world's most valuable dog. Masterpiece had run away twice in his life. When he was recovering from distemper in New Jersey, he disappeared into the woods for three days. He eventually returned, a bit dirty but otherwise no worse for wear. Another time, Masterpiece slipped out the door of Poodles, Inc. and curled up in a linen shop on Park Avenue.[14] He was returned to his owner later that day. Perhaps, experts thought, Masterpiece was simply sick of being in the limelight. He had run away from a life of stardom, and he wasn't coming back.

Then, a witness came forward with evidence. They claimed to have seen a fashionably dressed lady in a long, red coat walking out the front door of Poodles, Inc. with a gray toy poodle by her side. The witness said that normally, they wouldn't have noticed the woman—fashionable ladies with poodles walked out that door every day. But this poodle was different, because he wasn't on a leash. Masterpiece was a trained show dog, which meant that he had been taught to follow commands. The more Pulaski heard from this eyewitness, the more he began to believe that his dog had been stolen.[15]

But even after the witness came forward about the woman in red, nothing happened. The police had no other leads to follow—and they couldn't interview every woman in New York with a red coat. Months went by with no sign of Masterpiece. Somehow, one of the world's most well-known canines had simply disappeared.

REMEMBERING MASTERPIECE

Without Masterpiece, Poodles, Inc. was never the same. Pulaski kept the store open for a few more years but decided to close up shop in 1956. In the three years that the store operated without Masterpiece, newspapers reported that the showroom was like a shrine to the missing poodle.[16] Pulaski tried to train Johnny, Masterpiece's puppy, to take his father's place, but it wasn't the same. As reporters said, Masterpiece was a born star—but his offspring was "just Johnny."[17] Pulaski kept breeding his beloved poodles, but he never found another Masterpiece.

Alexis Pulaski lived to be 73 years old and achieved great success as a dog breeder and groomer. But in his brief obituary in the *New York Times*, Masterpiece is the star. It reads: "In 1953, a silver-gray male poodle named Masterpiece was stolen from the store and was never recovered. The dog was credited with having been the sire of more than 300 toy poodles, which sold for as much as $2,500 each."[18]

Experts at the American Kennel Club suspect that Pulaski would have been happy with this remembrance. Masterpiece was his greatest achievement. It makes sense that in the story of his life, the little dog would take up the most space.

The story of Masterpiece isn't just a mystery about a missing dog. It's also a story about the role that dogs play in our lives—and what kind of life we should give them. Was Masterpiece's fame and fortune the kind of life a dog would want? Maybe someone stole him—but maybe he just ran away from it all to spend his final years napping on a cheap sofa and eating kibble out of a plain, metal bowl. If Masterpiece was kidnapped, did someone take him because he was worth so much money? Or did the woman in the red coat steal Masterpiece simply because she wanted the companionship of an especially good dog?

Unfortunately, as Brynn White writes, "The world will likely never learn the fate of its most valuable dog ..."[19]

CHAPTER TWO

A THIEF IN THE DUTCH ROOM

On March 18, 1990, two men disguised as police officers walked up to the doors of the Isabella Stewart Gardner Museum in Brookline, Massachusetts, and pushed the buzzer. Normally, the museum is bustling with activity. Visitors from across the globe arrive each day to wander through the Gardner's stunning galleries, with their arched doorways and lush wallpaper covered in priceless artwork. But when the uniformed men approached the building on March 18, it was just after one o'clock in the morning. The museum's courtyard garden, which stretches four stories up to a ceiling made entirely of glass, was empty except for the shadowy figures of a few tropical plants, waiting patiently for the start of another busy day.

There were two guards on duty that night. Outside, they could see the silhouettes of what looked like two officers in the darkness. The purported officers said they were responding to a call about a disturbance at the museum. But the guards at the watch desk had been there all night. As far as they knew, there was no disturbance. One guard, Rick Abath, let the officers in anyway. They walked through the employee entrance to the watch desk and immediately demanded the guards step away from their desk. Then, they pulled out two pairs of handcuffs.

"Gentlemen," they said, "this is a robbery."[20]

In a matter of minutes, the guards were tied up in the museum's basement with duct tape over their mouths.

According to the Boston Public Library, most art heists are over in ten minutes.[21] But that night, the fake officers spent eighty-one minutes in the Gardner Museum. They cut eleven priceless paintings out of their gilded frames: one Vermeer, three Rembrandts, a Manet, a Flinck, and five paintings by Edgar Degas. They also stole an ancient Chinese wine cup and a bronze eagle ornament from Napoleon's French Imperial Army. Surveillance footage shows them loading their car not once, but twice.

As the guards sat helplessly in the basement, the thieves' movements were tracked by the museum's motion alarm system. "! SOMEONE IS IN THE DUTCH ROOM," the alarm transcript reads over and over again. "INVESTIGATE IMMEDIATELY!!!"[22]

But no one could investigate. By the time staff found the security guards at eight fifteen the following morning, the artwork, and the robbers, were long gone.

For more than thirty years, the Gardner Museum and FBI investigators on the case have been searching for the thirteen stolen artworks that disappeared that night. But they've never resurfaced. Now, experts are asking: Who were these thieves? And why have they been hiding thirteen priceless pieces of art for more than three decades?

SELLING VAN GOGH

Thieves are drawn to art museums because the museums are full of multimillion-dollar treasures. And, as the thieves at the Gardner Museum discovered, many of those treasures can be stuffed quite easily into the trunk of a car. But there's one problem with stealing art that many thieves overlook: It's one-of-a-kind. And that means it's very identifiable.

As professor and pop culture expert Robert Thompson says: "When you rob a bank you spend the money. When you steal jewelry you pawn it off. When you steal a car you drive it. But what do you do with a famous stolen painting?"[23]

What do thieves do with the precious art they take? The answer is complicated, but there are five common paths thieves can take to offload a stash of priceless paintings:[24]

1. Steal to Order

Smart thieves know that you can't just sell a Van Gogh after you take it from the Louvre. These are high-profile cases, and there are databases that keep track of stolen artworks so that thieves can't easily resell them. But savvy thieves might steal a work of art at the request of someone who wants it for their private collection. People with a couple million dollars to spare could hire a thief to break into a museum and take a priceless painting just so they can hang it in their living room.

2. Pretend It's Legal

If you act quickly, you might find success selling a painting legally through an auction house or art dealer. Museums have enormous collections that they keep in storage when they aren't on display, and many don't take regular inventory of those artworks. A thief could snag a painting from the back room and sell it to a dealer before a museum even notices it's been stolen.

3. Demand a Ransom

Museums want nothing more than to get their lost treasures back—which is why many thieves will steal art just to ransom it back to the very people they took it from. Right now, the Gardner Museum is offering $10 million to anyone who can provide information that will help investigators recover their thirteen lost artworks. So far, no one has come forward.

4. Collect the Insurance Money

If ransoming the art doesn't work, sometimes insurance companies will take the bait instead. Museums have insurance to cover damage and losses in their collection, which insurance companies pay out after an investigation is complete. After the insurance company pays for a stolen work of art, however, they own it. Chances are, it won't ever resurface—but if it does, the insurance company, not the museum, claims the piece. Because of this, most insurance companies have a no-questions-asked policy around returning stolen art. Crime professor Erin Thompson elaborates: "You can steal a painting and give it to your girlfriend to hand over to the insurers—she'll say she found it in a bus stop and you'll get around 10 to 15 percent of the value of the art."[25] There's only one problem with this plan: Most priceless artwork is too expensive for museums to insure. All the pieces that were taken from the Gardner, for example, were not covered by insurance.

5. Try the Black Market

If ransom doesn't work and the museum already knows the painting is gone, your options are limited—and that means you have to sell the art on the black market. But the black market isn't as lucrative as thieves would like to believe. That's because criminals are always tricking other criminals into buying fake paintings. As FBI art crime specialist Christopher McKeogh explains: "Individuals have been known to create fake versions of well-known stolen works. If a stolen artwork is discovered on a black market, there's a good chance it could be a fake."[26]

Who would want to buy stolen art on the black market, anyway? Mostly mobsters, as it turns out—and not because they love Degas. Investigators often trace stolen artwork back to people in crime rings who plan to use the stolen pieces to negotiate lighter prison sentences if they get caught. Which is why when thieves broke into the Gardner Museum, detectives immediately started poking around Boston's massive network of organized crime.

A LIFE OF CRIME

Boston has been a hotbed for organized crime since the early 1900s, when the Patriarca crime family was established—an Italian American mob family that still operates today in Rhode Island, Massachusetts, and Connecticut. For the last hundred years, the Patriarca family has worked alongside other criminal organizations, like Whitey Bulger's infamous Winter Hill Gang, the Anguilo family, and the Merlino gang. As news about the Gardner heist spread, FBI agents immediately started calling in the gangsters they knew best.

First on the suspect list was Whitey Bulger, a career criminal who was famous for wreaking havoc and pulling strings in Boston. FBI agent Thomas McShane investigated Bulger, but the man claimed he wasn't involved in the heist. In fact, he said, he sent his own men to figure out who did it, because he was angry they committed a crime on his turf without giving him a cut.[27] Bulger had a few connections that made him look suspicious—for example, he had ties to the Boston police, who might have given him access to real police uniforms. He was also known to associate with the Irish Republican Army, a mafia-like organization famous for its heists. Ultimately, though, after hours of questioning, McShane found no concrete evidence to connect Bulger to the crime.[28]

After ruling out Bulger, agents turned to another local crime ring: the Merlino gang. The gang, which operated out of the TRC Auto Electric auto body shop in Dorchester, was run by Carmello Merlino, who had connections with the Patriarca crime family. Merlino was known for high-profile robberies, and on a few occasions offered to exchange priceless stolen artwork for reduced jail time. But when he was caught for another robbery and questioned about the Gardner heist, Merlino claimed he was being set up.[29] He maintained that he didn't know anything about the lost art—and he seemed to be telling the truth.

But it's possible, FBI agents now believe, that one of his associates did know something.

David Turner, who worked for Merlino, has been linked with the Gardner heist since the beginning. Turner and a friend of his named George Reissfelder both worked at TRC under Merlino, where they quickly got wrapped up in organized crime. But the idea for the Gardner heist might not have been planted by Merlino himself. In the podcast *Last Seen*, WBUR reporters share that Reissfelder's boyfriend at the time (who was also a convicted criminal in Boston's underground crime network) suggested Turner and Reissfelder steal some priceless art because "the TRC gang was getting sloppy,"[30] and they might need some collateral to avoid going to prison.

Turner later told FBI agents that he had no idea who really did steal the Gardner's art—supposedly he was picking up drugs for Merlino in Florida that night and couldn't have committed the crime. But FBI agents have long wondered whether Turner faked his alibi. On the one hand, he looked a lot like sketches of one of the fake policemen. And on the other, he had ties to two other mobsters and prime suspects in the case—both of whom happened to be named Bobby.

THE BOBBYS

The current investigation into the Gardner Museum heist often comes back to the same two characters: Bobby Guarente and Bobby Gentile. But the Bobbys didn't become suspects until 2010—six years after Bobby Guarente died.

Guarente was a Boston mobster and longtime associate of the Merlino gang. Prime suspect David Turner thought of Guarente as a father figure, and Carmello Merlino walked Guarente's wife Elene down the aisle at their wedding.[31] Guarente had deep ties to some of the heist's suspected key players—but he didn't come to the FBI's attention until Elene started talking to agents one day in 2009.

The story, according to Elene, goes like this: In 2005, Guarente and Elene sat down for a seafood dinner with another career criminal, Bobby Gentile, and his wife in Portland, Maine. After dinner, the couples walked to the parking lot together, where Elene watched her husband give two of the Gardner paintings to Gentile. Supposedly, Guarente had been hiding the artwork in his house in Maine for years—though when FBI agents searched the home, they found no trace of the paintings.[32]

Who was Bobby Gentile, the man who supposedly took the Gardner art off Guarente's hands? According to FBI agents, Gentile was another Boston mobster who worked alongside Guarente in the 1990s. He was also still alive when Elene Guarente pointed the finger at him in 2010—which made him a prime target for the FBI. For more than a decade, FBI agents questioned Gentile repeatedly about information involving the Gardner heist. But every time they spoke with him, he denied involvement.

Despite Gentile's claims that he wasn't involved, the FBI thought Elene was a credible witness. So in 2010, they headed to Manchester, Connecticut, to search Gentile's house. They did a thorough search, using ground-penetrating radar to see if Gentile might have buried the priceless paintings. During that search, they found a typewritten page with a list of every piece of art that was stolen from the Gardner, along with its estimated value. But they found no trace of the art itself.[33]

Bobby Gentile died of a stroke in 2021. He was eighty-five years old, and one of the last living suspects in the Gardner Museum heist. But even though Gentile can't share his knowledge anymore, FBI agents haven't stopped gathering evidence. They learned from Gentile's cousin, Sebastian "Sammy" Mozzicato, a mobster who eventually became an FBI informant, that Gentile once offered to sell another gangster two Gardner paintings for half a million dollars each. But the purchaser got suspicious in the end and didn't go through with the deal. Mozzicato also claims that Gentile used to keep the Gardner's stolen bronze eagle statue in his auto body shop.[34] Meanwhile, yet another Bobby (mobster Bobby Luisi) claims that Bobby Guarente once told him that he buried the Gardner artwork under a concrete slab in Florida.[35]

If you ask criminal insiders, the Bobbys are promising suspects. But there's one major problem: Mobsters aren't reliable witnesses. According to Bobby Gentile, Elene Guarente once showed him the small, stolen Rembrandt sketch, which she kept inside her bra. "[Elene's] crazy. She's bipolar. She's nuts, I know she was nuts," Gentile said in his only TV interview about the crime.[36]

But reporter Edmund Mahoney thinks that Gentile is the one with something to hide. He told the film crew working on a Netflix documentary about the heist: "A guy like that, what are you gonna do—he's never told the truth in his life."[37]

EMPTY FRAMES

For thirty years, art investigators at the FBI have been hard at work trying to track down the thirteen pieces that were lost on March 18— and the men who took them. But in the world of organized crime, where everyone is trying to save themselves, it's impossible to know who to believe. Agents now think the stolen artwork was moved from Boston to Connecticut, and then down the Eastern Seaboard to Philadelphia. From there, the trail hits a dead end. But even now, after years of questioning mafiosos and tracking black-market deals, agents wonder: Was it an inside job all along?

As they made links between a string of notorious mobsters, FBI agents never stopped looking at the people closest to the crime. And one of the guards, Rick Abath, has been a person of interest in the case for years. On the night of the heist, then twenty-three-year-old Abath buzzed the officers in—which some people argue was the plan all along. Motion-sensor records also show that the thieves never entered the Blue Room, where one painting was stolen, during the eighty-one minutes they were inside. The last person to walk through the Blue Room (perhaps to remove a painting from the wall for the thieves before they arrived) was Rick Abath. The mystery of Abath's presence in the Blue Room has never been solved.[38]

Like so many other suspects before him, Abath has spent three decades defending his innocence. But unlike the mobsters in the interrogation room, Abath feels horrible about the loss of those thirteen pieces of art and the role he played in their disappearance. "Even if they get the paintings back they'll never be the same, and I feel horrible about that," he told NPR in 2015. "I don't want to be remembered for this alone ... but they're saying it's half a billion worth of artwork. And ultimately, I'm the one who made the decision to buzz them in."[39]

Today, most of the original suspects in the Gardner Museum heist are either dead or in prison. But a few people, like Abath, still remember what happened that night. Art experts, historians, and Gardner Museum staff are all still waiting for answers in one of the longest unsolved art heists in history. For now, though, all we have are eleven empty frames, which still hang in the Gardner Museum. They remind visitors who wander the galleries of that fateful March night—and the precious art that we lost so many years ago.

CHAPTER THREE

THE REAL GHOST BUSTERS

To be a part of the world's oldest ghost investigation organization, you don't have to believe in spirits. You just have to be open-minded.

"Our prime interest is that of paranormal phenomena associated with ghosts and hauntings," the Ghost Club website reports. "It should be stressed, that we do not perform clearances or exorcisms, and the use of Ouija Boards is strictly prohibited ... Our aim is to conduct serious research; our investigations are not for entertainment purposes or for thrill seekers."[40]

For the last 150 years, the Ghost Club has met in living rooms, lecture halls, parks, and pubs in London to try to explain the unexplainable. But to really understand the club, you have to go all the way back to 1848—to a little farmhouse in Hydesville, New York.

SPIRITS COME KNOCKING

Hydesville, New York, doesn't exist anymore. It was swallowed up by the neighboring town of Arcadia a long time ago. But back in 1848, it was a rural farming community, and the home of Kate and Maggie Fox.[41]

The Fox family lived in an old farmhouse that had a reputation around town for being haunted. The previous owners had complained about mysterious and unexplainable experiences in the house. But it wasn't until late March 1848 that the Fox family began to complain about bumps in the night. They said they heard sounds like tapping on the walls—and on some nights, it sounded as if the furniture was moving.

One afternoon, the two youngest Fox daughters approached their neighbor to tell her about a strange situation. According to fourteen-year-old Maggie and eleven-year-old Kate, the nighttime knocks weren't random after all. There seemed to be a spirit behind them. The curious woman followed the girls up to the bedroom. It was then that the show began.

"Count five," Margaret Fox, the girls' mother, said aloud. It appeared to the neighbor as if she was talking to no one at all.

But then, the rapping started. The woman listened in awe to five loud knocks.

"Count fifteen," Margaret said next. This time, the ghost knocked fifteen times.

Margaret asked the spirit to tell her how old the neighbor was, and the ghost knocked thirty-three times. Of course, the ghost was right.

Then, Margaret asked a final question. "If you are an injured spirit," she said, "manifest it by three raps."

And three knocks were heard in the Fox farmhouse.[42]

The neighbor and Margaret Fox were both horrified. And to their credit, Kate and Maggie seemed terrified, too. Soon after, the Foxes left the house abandoned, and the girls moved in with their older sister, Leah, who lived in nearby Rochester. But the story didn't end there. Two community leaders named Isaac and Amy Post heard about the knocking. There was a rumor around town that the ghost may have been the spirit of a man who was murdered in the old Fox house. The Posts invited Maggie and Kate to their house because they were curious. They wanted to know if the girls could channel spirits in other places, too.

All three of the Fox sisters showed up at the Posts' that night, and all three proved that they could speak with ghosts. Maggie and Kate communicated with a spirit who answered by thumping on the floor. Leah, the eldest sister, even claimed that she was talking with the ghost of the Posts' daughter, who had recently died. Word spread around the state: the Fox sisters could speak with people on the other side.[43]

The Fox sisters traveled across the United States and to England, sharing their gifts. And many other aspiring channelers got involved, too. It became popular to invite mediums, who claimed they could talk with the deceased, to dinner parties, where they would speak with long-dead inhabitants of the house. Eventually, the fad became its own religion: spiritualism.[44]

After the American Civil War, many families were grieving, and spiritualism became even more popular. Everyone wanted the chance to say goodbye to their dead loved ones, lost in distant battlefields. There was even a séance at the White House. Abraham and Mary Todd Lincoln invited a medium to try to speak with their son Willie, who died unexpectedly of tuberculosis.

Then, in 1888, the Fox sisters told the world the truth: They had made it all up. On stage in New York, Maggie and Kate admitted they used props to make thumping sounds. It was all an elaborate prank—one they didn't think would go this far. As Maggie said:

> My sister Katie and myself were very young children when this horrible deception began. At night when we went to bed, we used to tie an apple on a string and move the string up and down, causing the apple to bump on the floor, or we would drop the apple on the floor, making a strange noise every time it would rebound.[45]

But it didn't matter that Maggie and Kate had lied. By then, the ghost fever was everywhere. Although no one believed in the powers of the Fox sisters anymore, they definitely believed in spirits.

It was in this era of mediums, Ouija Boards, possessions, and hauntings that a group of professors at Trinity College in England started talking about the dead. These men were scholars and researchers, and they were beginning to wonder if the spooky stories they heard had any truth in them. They wondered if ghosts might exist after all.

And so, the Ghost Club was born.

A SUPERNATURAL SECRET SOCIETY

According to the Ghost Club website, the organization began in 1855, but it wasn't officially recognized until 1862. The earliest members of the club included curious clergymen, academics at Trinity College, and the author Charles Dickens. It was a secret society—you could only join if you received an invitation. Because of that, the members of the Ghost Club could share their strangest stories with each other without worrying about what other people might think.[46]

When Charles Dickens died in 1870, the club nearly went extinct. But a few devoted members started up the organization again in 1882. This new version of the Ghost Club was a bit less scientific than the version that Dickens had been a part of. Many club members were also famous mediums. On November 2, commonly known as All Soul's Day, the Ghost Club would gather to recite the names of all members, living and dead. After all, deceased members of the club were still an active part of the group. They were just tuning in from the spirit world.[47]

One famous member of the early Ghost Club was the poet W. B. Yeats. Yeats was one of many writers who joined the group over the years— but he was arguably the only one who believed that ghosts did his writing for him. Yeats and his wife, Georgina, would put their pencils on a piece of blank paper, and then take notes in a trancelike state. Yeats believed these notes were direct messages from the dead. Later in his life, Yeats claimed he learned many "lessons in Philosophy ... received from a group of beings on the other side."[48]

In 1993, more than one hundred years after the club was created, the members ran into trouble—and not the ghostly kind. The Ghost Club website reports: "After some turmoil at the club involving former presidents, it was decided to implement a more democratic feel to proceedings ..."[49] After years of being a secret, invitation-only society, the Ghost Club was going public. Unlike in the olden days, when a president led the proceedings, all members would now have a say in how the Ghost Club was run.

This transition also brought another important shift: ghosts were no longer the only topic of discussion. Members could now join the ranks if they were interested in dowsing, magic, cryptozoology (the study of creatures from folklore, like Bigfoot), and aliens. Today, any paranormal experience is fair game.

"THERE HAS TO BE SOMETHING"

At a pub in London, today's Ghost Club members meet to drink and share their spookiest stories. There are now 326 members of the club, spread across the world.

James Tacchi, an airplane pilot, is the technical advisor for the group. "If I were to ask my daughter [what a ghost is]," Tacchi says, "she'd paint a picture of a white sheet. But for me it's more an experience people have had that they can't explain. Is it a spirit of the dead? A religious manifestation? A hallucination? What was it they saw?"[50]

Most of the people in this pub are here because they have experienced something they can't explain—though some are just curious skeptics. Sarah Darnell, the club's secretary, worked for many years in hospitals and nursing homes where she saw patients die every day. "There were a lot of unexplained things that happened in my career," she says. "Shadows, whiffs of perfume, whispers of things that have come before—all of us who worked in the place saw and accepted these things."

"There are so many people who've had experiences they can't explain," Darnell adds. "There has to be something."[51]

What have the club members seen? Alan Murdie, the current club chairman, once saw the ghost of a woman he was in a relationship with for thirteen years appear in front of him. He found out two weeks later that on the same day he saw her spirit, she'd died.

James Tacchi remembers helping his dad, an electrician, work on wiring in a four-hundred-year-old pub. Upstairs, Tacchi heard furniture moving—and footsteps. Then, he heard a door open and shut. He called down to his dad that the owner of the pub had left. His dad looked up, confused. "The owner left an hour ago," he replied.

One of the most famous recent members of the Ghost Club, Andrew Green (1927–2004), spent more than six decades looking for spirits. He was so popular, in fact, that people called him "the Spectre Inspector." But the experience that started his journey into the paranormal was a terrifying one.

As a teenager in 1944, Green visited an old Victorian house with his father. The house was a storage facility for furniture from buildings that were bombed during World War II. Green went up into the tower of the house and found himself in front of a tall window. Suddenly, he felt the overwhelming urge to jump. In a kind of trance, he climbed to the ledge and prepared his leap. Thankfully, his father found him in time and dragged him back to safety.

Later, Green found out that many people had jumped from that tower in the past—many to their deaths. And when he returned to take a photo of the infamous window, the camera captured the face of a young girl. Decades earlier, in 1886, a girl had fallen to her death from that very ledge. Green was never able to explain how he captured that photograph of her face.[52]

THE LAST FRONTIER

Ghost hunters today have plenty of scientific equipment at their disposal: surveillance cameras, infrared sensors, and electromagnetic field recorders that many experts claim are the best way to find out that a spirit is present.

But for many Ghost Club members, the point isn't finding proof. The point is being free to wonder.

"People clump all things like this into fairy stories," says David Saunderson, a current Ghost Club member. "But several hundred years ago they didn't believe in electricity, even though we could see it in the sky ... We know there are things up there—radio waves, neutrinos, Wi-Fi—even if we can't see them. It's the spiritual part of the paranormal that gets dismissed. But science today was magic in the past."[53]

A member and cryptozoologist named Richard Freeman adds: "The mountain gorilla was dismissed as folklore until 1904. And the giant squid was filmed only recently. People don't believe until suddenly they do."[54]

The Ghost Club has never found concrete proof of a spirit. At least, not enough proof to convince modern scientists. But most of the members don't really care about that. They are just happy to have a space where they can ask questions and share their stories. Because the truth is, some things simply can't be explained by science—at least, not yet. We don't know who the girl was that Andrew Green saw in the window. We don't know what force slammed the door that scared James Tacchi.

So many of us have seen things we can't explain. But in those moments when logic fails us, there is a place where we can go. Where for more than 150 years, people have been sharing ghost stories—and trying to find answers to the questions science can't yet solve.

CHAPTER FOUR

THE CASE OF THE MISSING FEATHERS

At the Natural History Museum in the town of Tring, England, a guard cruised through the empty galleries. It seemed like a quiet night among the specimens. The halls of the museum were lined with millions of stuffed creatures—polar bears, sea turtles, kangaroos, the long-extinct dodo bird. Inside the display cases, millions of glassy eyes caught the beam of the guard's flashlight.

But it wasn't as quiet a night as the guard wanted to believe. In the office, an alarm beeped quietly. There was a broken window in one of the halls—and outside that window, a thin young man with a flop of hair over his eyes stood with a rolling suitcase in his hands.

That man was Edwin Rist. He was looking for feathers.[55]

Earlier that evening, Edwin Rist had left a performance at the Royal Academy of Music and taken a train forty miles northwest from London. It was late. Rist rolled his suitcase for an hour down the dark, sleepy roads that led to the center of town. Eventually, he found the road he was looking for—a small lane only about eight feet wide, lined with tall brick walls. On a map, it's Public Footpath 37, but locals call it Bank Alley.[56]

Rist slipped down the alley, clunking his suitcase behind him. He pressed his hands along the wall to find his way in the dark. Finally, he stopped. He looked up. In front of him was a wall topped with a roll of barbed wire. Beyond that was a small window. And beyond that window were millions of dollars' worth of precious, exotic feathers. Those feathers had been protected by curators for decades. They had come to Tring during World War II, when bombs were falling on London. Curators dodged German shells to pack these bird specimens carefully into boxes and move them to the quieter countryside in Tring.[57]

But Rist didn't care about that. All he cared about was the fact that after many months of planning, he had finally arrived.

Using a pair of wire cutters, Rist snipped the barbed-wire fence and heaved himself up onto the brick ledge. From there, he could barely reach the small window. Below him was nearly ten feet of empty air. If he fell, he would hurt himself—and alert the guard on duty that night.

But Rist didn't fall. Instead, he reached toward the windowpane and pulled out his glass cutter. He pressed the blade into the window, trying to make a hole big enough to slip through. But it wasn't as easy as it looked in the movies. He couldn't break through the thick pane. As he pressed and pressed, the cutters slipped from his hand and fell into the darkness below.[58]

Rist almost gave up then. This crazy plan, which had been months in the making, had gone too far. He was basically a kid, after all—only twenty years old.[59] What made him think he could rob a museum and get away with it?

But there was a voice in his head urging him along. The same voice that had sparked this wild scheme in the first place. "Wait a minute!" the voice shouted. "You can't give up now. You've come all this way!"[60]

Rist hopped down, grabbed a rock, heaved himself back up onto the ledge, and smashed through the window. Glass shattered and sprinkled onto the floor below.

He was in.

From here, Rist knew it would be easy. He pulled out a small flashlight and began to roll his suitcase through the halls. The museum was silent—though Rist had triggered an alarm, he didn't know it. And neither, it appears, did the guard on duty. Rist walked quietly through the galleries, past beautiful animals posing behind glass. Their mouths were open in a snarl. Their eyes seemed to follow him as he walked. But Rist wasn't interested in just any creature. He walked by.

Rist found his way to the vault. He knew this space intimately. Months earlier, he'd cased the museum by pretending to be a photographer working for a friend who was writing a PhD thesis on rare birds. He'd already spent hours inspecting the contents of this vault.[61] Inside were drawers and cabinets full of the precious specimens he was seeking: bird skins. He opened drawer after drawer to reveal brilliant feathers: red, blue, black, green, violet, gold. They were beautiful. They were perfect. And soon, they would be his.

Rist stuffed his suitcase full of the skins. He opened cabinet after cabinet, piling the contents into his rolling bag. In his mind, he ran through a list of names: cotingas, quetzals, fruitcrows, birds of paradise. He grabbed as many as he could carry, closed the drawers, zipped his suitcase shut, and emerged from the vault. A few moments later, he had slipped back through the broken window and into the unassuming night.[62]

Later that day, another guard walking through the museum noticed glass on the floor. He looked up and saw the shattered, jagged frame of the broken window. He ran to tell the curator, who immediately called the police. But when they arrived and started asking questions, the guard didn't have much to tell them.

"When was the window broken?" the police officer asked.

The guard looked up at the empty pane. He shrugged. "Sometime in the last twelve hours?" The guard hadn't noticed a thing.

Meanwhile, Mark Adams, the museum's senior curator responsible for bird skins, was frantically searching the collections for missing specimens. But all the cabinets containing the museum's most precious possessions were untouched. He examined the skeletons of the extinct dodo and great auk, the Galapagos finches collected by Charles Darwin himself. He stroked the cover of an original copy of John James Audubon's *Birds of America,* which had just sold at auction for $11.5 million and was considered the most valuable book in the world.

"Mercifully," author and researcher Kirk Wallace Johnson writes, "nothing seemed to be missing."[63]

If you asked the museum curators on that day, June 24, 2009, what happened, they would have told you that an intruder smashed the glass, searched the halls, and didn't find anything worth taking. The thief didn't know what he was looking at, they thought. They were lucky.

Meanwhile, back in his apartment in London, Rist was gazing over his collection of exotic bird skins: "twenty-four Magnificent Riflebirds. Twelve Superb Birds of Paradise. Four Blue Birds of Paradise. Seventeen Flame Bowerbirds."[64] All told, he was now the proud owner of 299 rare birds and nearly $1 million worth of feathers.

THREE HUNDRED BIRDS AND A NEW FLUTE

Why would a twenty-year-old boy steal 299 bird skins? That was the question that Kirk Wallace Johnson kept asking himself as he began to investigate the life and crimes of Edwin Rist. The answer, he eventually discovered, would take an unexpected turn into the world of fly-fishing.

Edwin Rist was born in a small town in upstate New York. He and his brother were homeschooled by their parents, who were both journalists. From an early age, Edwin was a talented musician. He particularly loved to play the flute, and he dreamed of becoming a professional flautist one day.

But the flute wasn't his only love. When he was ten years old, Edwin's father wrote an article for a magazine about the physics of fly-fishing—a particular kind of fishing done with colorful, often handcrafted hooks called flies. During his research, Edwin's father watched a video about the art of fly tying, and it captivated his two young sons. The flytier took a feather and pressed it in his fingers, and suddenly the hook was transformed into a work of art. In an interview with Johnson, Edwin recalls rummaging through his garage for a hook and some string so he could try it himself. He had found a new passion.[65]

Edwin's father noticed his sons' newfound interest in fly tying, and he took them both to a tackle shop to get supplies. Soon, both Rist brothers were competing in fly-tying competitions. The boys would spend hours crafting beautiful flies from feathers and string, designed to look like mayflies skimming the surface of the water.

Then, Edwin met a man named Edward "Muzzy" Muzeroll. Muzzy was a champion flytier with a particular area of expertise. He did Victorian salmon fly tying—a unique subset of normal fly tying that closely follows fly "recipes" from the 1800s—many of which rely on feathers from exotic, even extinct tropical birds. Edwin fell in love with Muzzy's flies, which were brilliantly colored and delicate works of art. A few months later, he was traveling to Maine to study under his new mentor.[66]

In Maine, Edwin sat through daylong workshops with Muzzy, who taught him not only the craft of salmon fly tying, but also its long history. Edwin followed the traditional recipes using substitute feathers, sometimes called "subs," instead of the expensive originals. Immediately, Muzzy noticed that Edwin had a knack for the art. At the end of their time together, Muzzy handed Edwin an envelope. Inside was about $200 worth of exotic feathers. "This is what it's really about," he told Edwin. Edwin nodded. From that day forward, normal feathers would never be enough.

By sixteen years old, Edwin was making a name for himself in both the music and fly-tying communities. But when it came to salmon fly tying, he had limitations: namely, money. Edwin would bid on exotic feathers on eBay and other websites, trying to get his hands on some originals. But he was always outbid by the wealthy, older tiers who had more money to spend.

"His devotion to this art form was ... always defined by a longing for what he didn't have," notes Johnson in an interview with radio producer Sean Cole.[67]

When Johnson asked Rist how he felt about using substitute feathers, he replied: "The knowledge of their falsity eats at you."[68]

Edwin grew up, and his musical talents took him to the Royal Academy of Music in London, where he trained to become a professional flautist. In one way, he was following his dreams. But privately, he still yearned for feathers. Then one afternoon, a fly-tying friend sent him a photo. It was an image of piles of beautiful, exotic birds. Apparently, Edwin's friend had visited a natural history museum outside London, in the small town of Tring. He'd gotten access to a private collection of rare bird skins from the mid-1800s, which weren't on display to the public.

Edwin knew immediately that he had to see those birds—though he didn't have the whole plot laid out in his mind quite yet. That came later, when he stood before one of the most precious collections of exotic birds in the world, looking hungrily at their bright tail feathers.

"He [realized then that he] would never have to wonder again where his next feather was coming from," says producer Sean Cole.[69]

CATCHING A BIRD THIEF

Back at the Natural History Museum in Tring, Detective Adele Hopkin had the same question as writer Kirk Wallace Johnson: "Why would someone want to steal a bunch of birds?"[70]

About a month after the discovery of the broken window in the gallery, one of the curators received a call from a researcher, who needed some information about a specimen. The curator opened the appropriate drawer in the vault. It was empty. He opened another drawer, and another.

Empty. Empty. Empty.

The police returned to the museum. This time, they were looking for evidence of a theft.

When Detective Hopkin showed up at the museum, she immediately suspected it might be an inside job. How else would so many specimens disappear without anyone noticing? But after a few interviews with staff members who were clearly devastated by the loss of the birds, that possibility seemed less likely. Plus, only a month before, the museum had reported a suspected break-in. Her initial theory wasn't adding up.

Hopkin hoped to find traces of an intruder on Tring's extensive network of security cameras, but unfortunately the footage is deleted every twenty-eight days—and it had been thirty-four since the robbery. But even without the cameras, she did find some other evidence. She conducted a thorough search of the broken window in the gallery and cast her eyes down into the gap between the brick wall and the windowsill. Then, something caught her eye. In a rain gutter, there was a latex glove, a glass cutter, and shards of broken glass. On one fragment of broken glass, Hopkin found blood. She bagged the evidence and sent it to the national forensic lab for testing. Now, all they could do was wait.[71]

And the police did wait—for almost a year. Without video footage or a hit on their blood sample, the police didn't have much to work with. Then, after months without a lead, a tip came in. A flytier at a convention in the Netherlands saw a bird skin for sale—nothing out of the ordinary. Except this bird looked familiar to him. He remembered a press release about the Tring museum heist from months before. He suspected this might be one of their birds.

With a tip in hand, the police started tracing that bird skin back to its source. Their hunt took them to an apartment in London. And in that apartment, they found Edwin Rist.[72]

When police showed up at his door, Edwin confessed immediately. He took them into his bedroom, where his girlfriend was still asleep. In the bedroom were dozens of beautiful birds—many with their bright feathers plucked and cut. Edwin was arrested on the spot.

Because Edwin confessed, he wasn't taken to trial. But if he had been, the police would have had plenty of evidence. Not only did Edwin hand over all the birds, he also had an eBay account tied to his name that showed every feather and bird skin he'd sold in the last year. One listing read, "Indian crow feathers for sale. Buying new flute."[73]

On Edwin's hard drive there was a Word document. It was named "Plan for Museum Invasion.doc."

Edwin was charged with burglary and selling stolen goods, which usually came with sentences of ten and fourteen years, respectively. But that's not the sentence Edwin got. His lawyers brought in a psychologist, who diagnosed Edwin with Asperger's syndrome, often known as high-functioning autism. In England, there are certain sentencing limitations for people with Asperger's syndrome, and the judge knew that if he gave Edwin the typical sentence, it would be appealed.[74] So instead, he sentenced Edwin to one year's suspended sentence and a hefty fine of 125,000 euros[75]—the amount of money law enforcement suspected he made selling the feathers. If he didn't pay the fine, he would have to serve his prison sentence.

At the end of the hearing, Edwin Rist was free to go. The missing birds were returned—or at least, the ones that the police could recover. About a third were safe and sound, and another third had been damaged or had feathers removed. The remaining third, according to author Kirk Wallace Johnson, were still missing.[76]

THE FEATHER UNDERGROUND

After Edwin was sentenced, the investigation was over. But Kirk Wallace Johnson couldn't help feeling unsatisfied about the ending. A person had stolen dozens of hundred-year-old specimens, many of which were the only remaining evidence in the world of long-extinct tropical bird species. And he had basically gotten away with it.

To say it in Edwin's own words: "The fact that essentially an idiot with a rock could steal a suitcase full of birds from the natural history museum ... it's absurd."[77]

On top of that, no one was looking for the nearly sixty-four missing bird skins that hadn't been recovered by police. The curators in Tring had a detailed list of the missing birds—but there was no one willing to investigate.

No one, that is, except Johnson.

Johnson had a feeling that someone—perhaps even Edwin—was still selling those missing birds on the black market. He thought Edwin might have an accomplice. So he started searching for clues.

After hunting through forums, scrolling through long-gone eBay listings, and asking Edwin himself in an interview in London, Johnson came up with a list of potential suspects. But he didn't find any answers until he consulted with Rick Prum, an evolutionary ornithologist at Yale University. Prum has an impressive career in the sciences—but there's one mystery he's especially keen to solve. He wants to know who has those missing bird skins.

Prum and Johnson compared notes, which included a hunt through screenshots of Edwin Rist's old website. On that website, they found the clue they needed: evidence that traced Edwin to another eBay seller named "Goku."[78]

For years, Goku sold feathers and sometimes whole bird skins on eBay, just like Edwin. And for someone with a keen eye, it was clear that those birds came from Tring. After some sleuthing, Johnson discovered that the account was owned by a man in Norway named Long Nguyen. Nguyen was friends with Edwin. He was a flytier. This was the break Johnson needed.

Johnson wrote to Nguyen, asking for an interview. And to his surprise, Nguyen agreed. At Nguyen's home in Norway, Johnson was greeted by a chatty parrot, who spent most of the interview chewing on Johnson's ear.

In his interview, Nguyen admitted that he sold feathers for Edwin. But he didn't have the missing birds. And it was pretty clear from the start that he wasn't the criminal mastermind Johnson was looking for. He was a refugee from Vietnam who learned how to tie flies in a home for boys in Norway. He was kind and open. And, he admits, he wasn't interested in Edwin because of his feathers. He was just lonely after so many years living alone in a foreign country without his family. He was looking for a friend.[79]

Nguyen says that Edwin reached out to him to ask him to sell some feathers he "found." Johnson reports: "Long thought that that was what being a friend was. He thought he was going to help Edwin make enough money to buy his new flute. And he also felt really flattered and honored that Edwin Rist was paying attention to him."

"My assumption is just like he wanted to erase his traces. But the traces were already there, so I don't know why," Nguyen said in his talk with Johnson.

"But he's using you as a friend," Johnson replied.

"Yeah," Nguyen replied. "Yeah."[80]

"THAT BIRD IS GONE"

Johnson didn't find any missing birds that day—or any other day. At least, not yet. But he'll keep looking. Not because he wants to get back at Edwin Rist or any of the other flytiers who buy feathers on the black market. But because he cares about these birds.

"You can't go back and get another bird from 1860," Johnson tells producer Sean Cole. "That bird is gone."[81]

For Edwin, these birds were just a means to an end. They were supplies for his art—and a way to fund a new flute. But for scientists, these bird specimens are the only evidence they have of lost species and lost habitats. John McCormack, lab director at the Moore Lab of Zoology in Los Angeles, which houses more than 65,000 bird specimens like the ones Edwin stole, notes: "[These birds are a] snapshot in time from before pristine habitats were destroyed for logging and agriculture ... These skins hold answers to questions [scientists] have not yet thought to ask."[82]

Now, thanks to Edwin Rist, those answers are gone for good.

CHAPTER FIVE

ESCAPING ALCATRAZ

On the morning of June 12, 1962, one of the guards at the Federal Penitentiary at Alcatraz Island yelled at John Anglin, inmate AZ1335, to wake up. But he didn't wake up. The guard opened the cell door and approached John's bed. When he still didn't move, the guard shook John, trying to rouse him. That's when John's head rolled off the bed and onto the cement floor.[83]

The head was not actually John Anglin's head, of course. It was a very convincing papier-mâché dummy head. It was painted to look just like John—it even had a full head of real human hair, with eyebrows and long, thick eyelashes.

By then the real John Anglin, along with his brother Clarence and fellow inmate Frank Lee Morris, was long gone.

The night before, at around 10:30 p.m., the three men gathered around a small vent in their cell walls. Months earlier, they had created hidden passages by making small holes around the vents in each of their cells with a homemade drill they crafted out of a vacuum cleaner motor. They removed the false walls and slipped through the vents, as they had hundreds of times before. Every night for the last three months, they had taken this path to their secret workshop deep in the walls of Alcatraz prison. Tonight, they were visiting that workshop for the very last time.

In the workshop, the men had prepared all the supplies they would need for their journey. Three life vests made from stolen raincoats.

A 6 x 14-foot life raft made from more than fifty of those same raincoats. A set of wooden paddles. A hand pump, made from an accordion, which they would use to inflate their raft and vests. The remnants of a homemade periscope, so one of the men could keep watch for passing guards in the hall below.

The ceiling in their workshop was nearly thirty feet high, but that didn't stop them. The men climbed up a network of pipes to a ventilator shaft in the ceiling, which they had unlatched weeks earlier and kept open with a small piece of soap. They took turns dragging the life raft, vests, and paddles into the ventilator shaft. From there, the men climbed onto the roof, where they looked out over the dark, churning waters of San Francisco Bay.[84]

They were so close to freedom.

The men shimmied down a smokestack with their raft and paddles in tow, and then they climbed over a fence and onto the beach on the northeast shore of the island. They inflated their raft and life vests, climbed onto their makeshift boat, and launched into the frigid Pacific.

John, Clarence, and Frank turned toward Angel Island. They never looked back.

The next morning, guards discovered papier-mâché heads where three men should be—and a large hole in their cell walls. But by then, it was too late. The prison guards called in the FBI and the US Marshalls. But unlike every other escape attempt from that infamous island prison, these three men were never seen again. The bodies of John, Clarence, and Frank were never found—and for decades since, the US government has been trying to figure out what happened to the only three prisoners to ever escape from Alcatraz Island without getting caught.[85]

SMALL CRIMES, BIG ESCAPES

Before John and Clarence Anglin were famous prison escapees, they were just two poor, Southern brothers with a habit of getting into trouble. In fact, by most accounts, the Anglins weren't very good criminals at all.

John and Clarence moved around often as kids. Marie Anglin Widner, John and Clarence's sister, explained that their father worked as a migrant farmhand. The family moved to Florida in the winter to pick tomatoes, and then spent summers in Michigan harvesting cherries and strawberries.[86]

The family didn't have much money, but John and Clarence had other ways of keeping themselves occupied. The boys had a knack for finding trouble—whether they were chasing the neighbor's piglets or stealing tires and tractor batteries. As they got older, the trouble grew with them. By their early teens, John and Clarence were hot-wiring cars to cruise around town.

It was one of these incidents that landed Clarence in his first juvenile detention center. When he was fourteen, he spent a year in the Industrial School for Boys in Marianna, Florida—a place that was notorious for its violence. After he got out, he and John broke into a store and got caught again. That landed both boys in the school for another year.

As adults, John and Clarence were known for causing mischief—and for getting caught. Widner remembers just how bad they were at getting away with whatever trouble they got into. The men were sent to prisons all over the South for petty crimes. And every time they ended up in prison, they made plans to escape. In fact, some records show that John and Clarence managed to escape from every single prison they were placed in.[87]

"Sometimes, they'd just walk home," Widner told reporter Phoebe Judge. "They missed our mama's cooking."[88]

But the final straw for Clarence and John came in 1958, when the men robbed the Bank of Columbia, in Columbia, Alabama, with their older brother, Alfred. The three brothers entered the bank brandishing toy guns. They were later caught in Cincinnati and sentenced to thirty-five years for their crime.[89]

Widner reports that during the robbery, an older woman started to faint from fear. Alfred, the oldest brother, stopped the holdup to get the woman a glass of water.[90] Afterward, John used the money from the robbery to buy their mother an electric washing machine.

The Anglin brothers were all sent to a prison in Atlanta, but John and Clarence wouldn't stop trying to escape. The prison administration didn't know what to do with them, so they shipped them off to Leavenworth, Kansas. But just a few months later, John tried to smuggle Clarence out of Leavenworth prison in a large box that had once been used to deliver bread.

It was the last straw. John and Clarence Anglin were on their way to Alcatraz.

"ESCAPE PROOF"

Alcatraz Island is often referred to as "The Rock" in popular culture, and that's exactly what it is—a large hunk of stone sticking out of the water about a mile from San Francisco. The island has no native vegetation or animal life. For many decades, it was a military fortress, and then a military prison. But for twenty-nine years, from 1934 to 1963, the island was the most notorious maximum-security prison in America.[91]

The claim to fame of Alcatraz Island was that it was "escape proof." The fortress was surrounded by freezing cold water. The water temperature in San Francisco Bay rarely reaches 60 degrees Fahrenheit, even in the summer.[92] San Francisco Bay is also known for having strong, violent tides—promising an untimely end for any swimmers who dare to test the waters.

During the three decades that Alcatraz was operational, it housed some of the most well-known criminals in American history, including Al Capone, Whitey Bulger, and Alvin Karpis.[93] But not all the island's 1,500 inmates were violent gangsters. Many of them were just troublemakers who refused to follow the rules at other prisons. When the guards didn't know what to do with an inmate anymore, they sent them off to Alcatraz.

Because of its reputation, many of the prisoners at Alcatraz were known escape artists. In fact, in its thirty-year history, the prison experienced fourteen escape attempts involving thirty-six men. In all those attempts, not a single prisoner succeeded—they were either caught or died in San Francisco Bay.[94] It's unclear whether John and Clarence knew this when they started planning their escape with Frank Lee Morris and Allen West.

The Anglin brothers already knew both Frank Morris and Allen West from previous stints in prison. Frank Morris was another lifelong resident of the prison system. He was a foster kid who was shuffled between families from the time he was a baby. He started committing petty crimes when he was in middle school, and he was convicted for the first time when he was only thirteen years old. By the time he was eighteen, he had been charged with everything from armed robbery to drug possession. Like the Anglins, he knew what it was like to have spent most of his life in a cell.[95]

The other inmate, Allen West, was also an old acquaintance of John Anglin's. They met at the state penitentiary in Florida. West claimed that he was the mastermind behind the great escape. He says the plot began when he found old saw blades in a utility closet that the men could use to craft the various tools they'd need to escape. But it's hard to know if West is telling the truth, because he was known for being arrogant—and he was the only insider left to tell the tale. On the night of the escape, West claimed that he couldn't remove the vent in his cell. Everything we know now about the only successful escape in the history of Alcatraz Island comes from the mouth of the one man who was left behind.[96]

THE SEARCH

After discovering the escape, prison officials immediately called in the FBI. Agents began their manhunt—but they didn't find much in the way of clues. In the days following the disappearance, only a few items surfaced from the murky waves: a paddle, a life jacket, and a sealed packet of letters belonging to one of the Anglin brothers.[97] None of those clues gave agents any indication whether the men were dead or alive.

For seventeen years, the FBI stayed on the case. And for all those years, they didn't find a single hint that might indicate the men's whereabouts. Ultimately, they decided that the men couldn't possibly have survived the escape, based on four primary reasons:

1. Though the swim from Alcatraz to Angel Island is only a mile, the water is frigid and the currents are strong. If the men ended up in the water, it's unlikely they would have survived.

2. Allen West told agents that the plan, once the men made it to Angel Island, was to steal a car and some clothes. But no thefts of this kind were reported to the police after the incident. If the men made it to land, how did they leave San Francisco without being spotted?

3. The men didn't seem to get any help from their families. Frank Lee Morris had no living family members, and the Anglin family didn't have the means to support Clarence and John.

4. For nearly two decades, no credible evidence surfaced to prove that the men were alive.[98]

But not everyone believes that John, Clarence, and Frank died in San Francisco Bay. Marie Anglin Widner is certain her brothers escaped with their lives.

"I don't have any doubts that they did get out. No, I don't have any doubts. Never have," says Widner.[99]

Widner, who is now in her eighties, has many reasons to believe her brothers are still alive. For one, she says, they were always strong swimmers. As kids, John and Clarence used to swim for miles across the lake near their house. Widner remembers that in Michigan, they would even break the ice to go for a dip in the middle of winter.

Widner also has other evidence. Reputable people in her community have claimed to see the Anglin brothers over the years. At her mother's funeral, the men were supposedly seen dressed in women's clothing. And when their father died, Widner says, two strangers with long beards wearing strange hats and long overcoats showed up at the funeral home two hours before the service and asked to see the casket. The Anglin family never found out who the men were—but they had their suspicions.[100]

Alfred—John, Clarence, and Marie's eldest brother—also factors into the saga. In 1962, Alfred was in prison in Alabama. But a few weeks after the great escape, Alfred got a package in the mail. It was a small leather pouch with a horse on it. Widner still has that pouch, and she claims that the stitching matches the stitching on a leather wallet Clarence made years before. Inside the pouch, Widner says, there was a blank sheet of paper. But Alfred knew that the page wasn't actually blank. As kids, the boys had sent each other secret notes by writing in milk, and then setting the paper on fire. In the flames, hidden letters appear.

In his prison cell, Alfred took a match and lit that paper on fire. He held it over the toilet as it burned, and it revealed the true whereabouts of his two brothers.

But before Alfred could tell Marie their secret, he died. He tried to escape only a few months later and was electrocuted on a fence surrounding the prison. To this day, Marie has no idea what the note said.[101]

There's one other person who up until very recently was still looking for John, Clarence, and Frank: Deputy US Marshal Michael Dyke.

When the FBI closed their investigation, they turned the search for the fugitives over to the US Marshals. And the marshals will continue to look for a missing fugitive for decades—no matter how cold the case. According to Dyke, the marshals will search for the Anglins and Morris until the men are ninety-nine years old.

After that, he says, they'll cut them some slack.

Dyke is now retired, but in the years that he was assigned to the case, he familiarized himself with the FBI files and subsequent investigations by the marshals. And in the last decade, there have been some significant developments in the case. In 2015, a picture surfaced of two men standing in front of a termite mound in Brazil. Based on their clothing, the photo appears to have been taken around 1975. The men appear to be John and Clarence Anglin. The US Marshals hired an expert to use facial recognition software to determine whether the men were actually the Anglin brothers, but the results were inconclusive.[102]

Other bits of evidence also support the theory that the men have been hiding from the law for all these years. Christmas cards were sent to family decades later that matched the brothers' handwriting. One Anglin sibling also made a deathbed confession that John and Clarence had been in touch often from 1963 until 1987.

There's also the fact that in 2013, a man claiming to be John Anglin got in touch with the US government. His note read, in part:

> My name is John Anglin. I escaped from Alcatraz in June 1962 with my brother Clarence and Frank Morris. I'm 83 years old

and in bad shape. I have cancer. Yes we all made it that night but barely![103]

The letter went on to say that Frank died in 2008 and Clarence in 2011. The writer claiming to be John said that he would be willing to reveal his location if the US government would agree to give him a one-year prison sentence, during which he could receive medical treatment. The FBI analyzed the letter using fingerprint and handwriting analysis but was never able to prove it belonged to John.

A WHITE HOUSE ON A MOUNTAIN

Marie Anglin Widner doesn't know if her brothers survived or if they are still alive—but that doesn't mean she's given up hope. For years, Widner says, she had dreams that her brothers were living in a big white house on the side of a mountain. And that's where she pictures them now, six decades later.

"I'm still waiting," Widner says.[104]

And while she waits, Widner and her family keep the memory and legacy of the Anglin brothers and Frank Lee Morris alive. After all, it's not every day that a person escapes from Alcatraz.

CHAPTER SIX

THE SEARCH FOR AGATHA CHRISTIE

On December 4, 1926, Agatha Christie kissed her daughter Rosalind goodnight. Then, she packed a small suitcase, hopped in her Morris Cowley roadster, and disappeared into the foggy winter evening. By the following day, the famous novelist would be gone.[105] She left behind only three letters and an abandoned car with a bottle of poison in the back seat.

What happens when a writer known for her twisted plots disappears without a trace? Was her disappearance intentional—or was she the victim of a horrible accident?

To find out, police and searchers had to follow the clues that Agatha left behind.

WHO WAS AGATHA CHRISTIE?

Agatha Christie was born in Torquay, a sleepy little seaside town in Devon, England, in 1890. Her childhood was a happy one, thanks to her loving parents, Frederick and Clarissa Miller. The family wasn't wealthy, but they were comfortable. Agatha spent her early years surrounded by family, gazing across the English Channel to France and whatever lay beyond it.

Agatha always assumed that one day she would find the perfect husband and live happily ever after. And she was sure that she'd found that man when she met Colonel Archibald Christie, a military pilot. Agatha fell in love with Archie because he was adventurous. She knew he would fill her life with excitement. And Archie was in love with her, too. Only two months after they met, he asked Agatha to marry him. Archie and Agatha were engaged.[106]

But even though Agatha dreamed of love and romance, her engagement was not very happy at all. From the beginning, Agatha's mother had a bad feeling about Archie. She knew Agatha was sensitive and thought Archie wasn't compassionate enough for her daughter. She also had a sneaking suspicion he might not be loyal to his wife. Agatha's mother meant more to her than anyone, and it was hard to see her mother doubt the man she loved. When World War I broke out in 1914 and Archie was sent to France, the two finally married. Nobody on either side of the family was happy with the arrangement. After the wedding, Archie went to war, and Agatha went back home to Torquay.

At home, Agatha helped around the house and worked as a nurse for the Torquay Town Hall Red Cross Hospital. She also worked at the hospital pharmacy, where she dispensed medicines. This experience would teach her all about the poisons her fictional criminals would use to commit horrible crimes.

Agatha started reading detective stories around this time because she found them soothing. The puzzles distracted her from thinking about the war. But she didn't begin writing her own stories until her older sister Madge made her a bet. Madge said that Agatha couldn't write a detective story where the reader is given all the same clues as the detective but is unable to figure out who did it. Inspired by the challenge, Agatha started writing The Mysterious Affair at Styles.[107]

Agatha realized while writing her first novel that she wanted to be an author. But she wasn't an instant success. After the war, she and Archie were very poor. Her first novel was rejected five times in two years. It wasn't until 1919 that Agatha finally got a call from a publisher about *The Mysterious Affair at Styles*. It was a slow start for her, but soon Agatha became famous for her quirky detectives: the mustachioed Hercule Poirot and unexpectedly sharp Miss Marple.

Even after Agatha's career took off, however, things were hard at home for the Christies. Agatha was often lonely and sad, and she got into fights with her husband and publisher. In 1926, the couple decided to see if country life would fix their problems. They moved out of London and into a beautiful Tudor house in Sunningdale, Berkshire. They named the house Styles, after Agatha's first book.

The Christies didn't know then that Styles was haunted—not by ghosts, but by bad luck. Every previous owner had experienced a horrible tragedy while living there. And soon, the Christies would join them. Styles would become the setting for the worst year of their lives.[108]

THE CLUES

On the morning of December 5, the police in Guildford got a call about an abandoned car. The Morris Cowley roadster was so close to the edge of a chalk quarry that only a hedge kept it from falling into the pit. Inside the car was a small briefcase, a torn-up postcard, a fur coat, some children's books, the end of a loaf of bread, and a small medicine bottle that read "poison lead and opium."[109] The car belonged to Agatha Christie.

The police immediately started searching for the lost novelist. First, they contacted her husband, Archie. Apparently, he hadn't been at home the night before—a detail that interested the police. Then, Agatha's secretary came forward with another clue. Agatha had left her a note the night before, which read: "I must get away. I cannot stay in Sunningdale much longer."[110]

The police searched for three days. But there was no sign of Agatha. None of her friends knew where she was, and she hadn't gone home to Torquay. The police interviewed Archie Christie, who claimed that his wife was having a nervous breakdown. Earlier that year, her beloved mother had died. Agatha hadn't been the same since, he said. He didn't seem particularly worried about his wife. The police began to wonder if something was going on at Styles that Archie didn't want them to know about.

Three days later, the police called off their search. Another clue had emerged. Agatha's brother-in-law had received a letter from her in the mail. It said that she was going to a spa in Yorkshire for "rest and treatment."[111] Just as quickly as it began, the mystery was solved.

Or was it?

THE SEARCH CONTINUES

Two days later, there was still no sign of Agatha. The police were starting to wonder if the letter to Agatha's brother-in-law was a trick to throw them off the trail. What if she had committed suicide and didn't want anyone to find her? What if something even more nefarious had happened—and Archie didn't want the police to know about it?

The hunt for Agatha Christie began again—and this time, it was bigger than ever. Three different police departments banded together to find her. They brought more than five hundred officers into the fields of Berkshire. They got airplanes to search the countryside. They even brought dogs to sniff out her scent.[112]

As the search continued, the whole country became fascinated by Agatha's disappearance. Where had she gone? Could a woman truly drive off one night and disappear forever? Or was this mystery novelist the victim of a crime just like the ones in her books? At one point, ten thousand to fifteen thousand citizens banded together to search the rolling hills of Berkshire, often called the Downs, for Agatha.[113]

There were moments during the eleven-day-long search that sparked curiosity. On December 10, Archie Christie was interviewed by the *Daily Mail* about his wife's disappearance. He said, "It is quite true that my wife had discussed the possibility of disappearing at will. Some time ago, she told her sister, 'I could disappear if I wished and set about it properly.'"[114] After this interview, people began to suspect that Agatha wasn't missing at all, that this was just a publicity stunt to sell her next novel. She would make herself disappear to prove just how well she could fool her readers.

But that wasn't the only theory. Some people claimed they saw Agatha walking through London dressed as a man. Someone else spread a rumor that Agatha was dead and had left behind a sealed envelope that could only be opened when her body was found. That envelope would reveal the entire mystery. Other people started searching through Agatha's manuscript in progress, looking for clues about her disappearance.[115] Even famous novelists like Dorothy L. Sayers and Sir Arthur Conan Doyle got involved in the great woman hunt.[116]

Meanwhile, the police focused their attention on two places. First, they searched a local pond called the Silent Pool. Local legend claimed that the pond was bottomless. People could disappear into it without a trace. The police sent divers into the dark pond, but they did not find Agatha.

The second place the police focused their attention was on Colonel Archibald Christie. They had a feeling he knew more than he would admit. Privately, they wondered if he was responsible for Agatha's disappearance.

But, at the end of the day, all these theories were just that—theories. None of them led the police to Agatha.

A WEEK AT THE SPA

Meanwhile, at the Harrogate Hydro spa in Yorkshire, England, one guest wasn't like the others. Rosie Asher was working as a chambermaid at the hotel at the time. Decades later, she reported:

> I didn't dare let on at the time ... I just went about my normal business. She had only one small case but said her luggage was coming along later. I thought it all a bit odd. I started putting some [news]papers on the table when I saw some pictures of this person. I noticed right away she had unusual-looking shoes and handbag. I thought: I've seen those somewhere before. Then it dawned on me.[117]

In the end, it was Agatha's black, buckled shoes and zippered purse that gave her away. Rosie Asher told a few men playing in the band about her suspicions that the mysterious guest was actually the famous novelist in disguise. They gossiped about the news with their wives. Eventually, the two musicians went to the police and reported Agatha's location. They did it because one of their wives, Nora Tappin, said she would report it if they didn't.[118]

At first, the police didn't believe that after all their searching, their missing person had been staying at a comfortable spa in Yorkshire under a fake name. Her note had been true after all.

As soon as Agatha was found, the police stopped their investigation into Archie Christie—who at the time was a prime suspect for murder. Archie went down to the spa and identified his wife, who was supposedly too disoriented and confused to speak with authorities. Agatha finally returned home, and the people of England waited to hear more. What really happened? Why did Agatha disappear? Why did she use the fake name Teresa Neele when she was staying at the hotel? And, after more than a week of searching and rumors and newspaper articles, why wasn't she or Archie saying anything about it?[119]

HUNTING FOR THE TRUTH

A few days after Agatha returned home, Archie Christie finally made a formal statement about what happened to his wife. According to the family doctor, he said, she was suffering from "a complete loss of memory and identity." Agatha, he explained, "does not know who she is."[120]

Agatha didn't remember what happened. That meant no one would ever know what caused her to abandon her car, take a train to Yorkshire, and disappear under a fake name while half of England looked for her.

It seemed like a simple explanation. But the public wasn't so sure.

For a while, everything was quiet in the Christie household. Agatha continued writing books. And then, two years later, the Christies appeared in the news again. Agatha was filing for divorce.

As it turns out, Archie had fallen in love with another woman—and just before Agatha disappeared, he had asked to end their marriage. His lover's name was Nancy Neele. She was a friend of Agatha's.

When the news came out, reporters finally got a chance to ask Agatha what happened that night. She told one reporter for the *Daily Mail*:

> ... [T]here came into my mind the thought of driving into [the pit]. However, as my daughter was with me in the car, I dismissed the idea at once. That night I felt terribly miserable. I felt that I could go on no longer. I left home that night in a state of high nervous strain with the intention of doing something desperate. ... When I reached a point on the road which I thought was near the quarry, I turned the car off the road down the hill toward it. I left the wheel and let the car run. The car struck something with a jerk and pulled up suddenly. I was flung against the steering wheel, and my head hit something. Up to this moment I was Mrs. Christie.

It was the same story that Archie had told two years earlier. Agatha was so confused and heartbroken that she drove her car into the chalk pit, hit her head, and lost her memory. It was also the only time she would ever talk about her disappearance with the public. Even in her autobiography, there is a gap. Eleven missing days that mark the end of her life with Archie Christie, her first love.

Eventually, Agatha Christie married an archaeologist named Max Mallowan, and she became one of the most famous and beloved mystery novelists of all time. But even though she wrote more than eighty mystery novels, the biggest mystery in her own life remained unsolved. As author Kate Weinberg says, "In her stories, the character of each and every person in the room was exposed. In her life, she left us guessing."[121]

What was Agatha thinking as she drove down that dark country road? Some experts believe she really did experience amnesia. Perhaps her mother's death and the end of her marriage in the same year were just too much for her to handle.

But other people, like the authors Jared Cade and Kate Weinberg, think Agatha always knew the true story of her missing eleven days. She just didn't feel the need to share her secret with the world.

After all, aren't we all entitled to our secrets?

CHAPTER SEVEN

SHERLOCK HOLMES AND THE FAIRY PHOTOGRAPHS

In the words of the great detective Sherlock Holmes: "When you have eliminated the impossible, whatever remains, however improbable, must be the truth."[122]

But what happens when the "truth" reveals a hidden world—one full of fairies, gnomes, and mythical beasts?

For Sir Arthur Conan Doyle, the writer who created Sherlock Holmes, that question would launch an investigation that would rival the expert sleuthing of his famous fictional detective. It would lead him all the way to Yorkshire, where he would get to know two teenaged girls with vivid imaginations—and a secret they would keep for more than fifty years.

FAIRIES COME TO COTTINGLEY

Our story begins during World War I in the small town of Cottingley, England, when young Frances Griffiths shows up at the Wright family's door with a suitcase and no idea when she'd return home. Her father, whom she lived with in South Africa, was fighting in the war, and he sent young Frances to England to live with her aunt and uncle while he was on the front. For a few years, Frances became part of the Wright household, spending hours playing in the family's large garden with her thirteen-year-old cousin Elsie.[123]

One afternoon in July 1917, nine-year-old Frances returned from the garden with soaking-wet shoes. Her aunt asked angrily how she managed to make such a mess, and Frances explained that she had been playing with fairies in the nearby stream. Elsie, who was always quick to defend her young cousin, came to her rescue. She insisted that Frances was telling the truth about the fairies, and that both girls had seen them near the stream. When Elsie's father looked at her skeptically, she asked to borrow his camera. Then, she dragged Frances into the garden to find proof.[124]

When the photos from Elsie and Frances's jaunt in the garden were developed, the Wrights were shocked. The picture shows Elsie sitting in the grass surrounded by four prancing fairies. She has a flower wreath in her hair, and the fairies are dancing around her, with small musical instruments in their hands and delicate, butterfly-like wings.

But Mr. Wright still wasn't convinced. He assumed the girls had somehow manipulated the picture. He asked them why the photo appeared to have "bits of paper" in it.[125] Elsie and Frances were disappointed—but they wouldn't stop there. A few weeks later, they borrowed the camera again. This time, the photo they took depicts Elsie on the lawn with a gnome beside her. He has a strange, hooked jaw and long, spindly legs. She is holding her hand out to the little creature, and he appears to be climbing into her lap.[126]

Dr. Merrick Burrow, who recently curated an exhibit on the Cottingley fairy photos, told the BBC: "I do not think anybody [in the Wright family] really believed it. But they couldn't explain how it had been done either."[127]

A few years passed, and nothing happened. The fairy photos were just a funny family story. No one could explain how Frances and Elsie created them. But in 1919, Mrs. Wright started to think about the photos again. She didn't necessarily believe they were real—but she didn't know for sure that they were fake, either. She brought the pictures to the Theosophical Society of Bradford, which was meeting that night to debate the possible existence of fairies. When Mrs. Wright showed the pictures to the society's president, Edward Gardner, he was amazed. He believed the photos were real. Not only that: they were the proof he needed to make his case that supernatural creatures were all around us, if we simply seek them out.[128]

In 1920, Gardner gave a lecture on the Cottingley fairy photographs in London. And it was at that lecture that the pictures came to the attention of the esteemed author Sir Arthur Conan Doyle. Conan Doyle was a committed spiritualist—and at that exact moment, he was working on an essay about fairies. When Conan Doyle saw the pictures of Elsie and Frances, he knew it was time to investigate.[129]

A DETECTIVE IN TOWN

Conan Doyle was best known for writing the Sherlock Holmes stories, and in those stories, his detective was observant and rational, with an almost superhuman ability to draw conclusions about people and events based on scraps of evidence. But Conan Doyle himself wasn't nearly as rational as his storybook detective. In his personal life, he was a committed spiritualist—a person who believes we can communicate with spirits and other supernatural beings. In fact, he once ended his longtime friendship with the famous escape artist Harry Houdini over an argument about whether his wife, Lady Doyle, had channeled the voice of Houdini's dead mother.[130]

Experts often claim that Conan Doyle became interested in spiritualism in 1918, after his son Kingsley died unexpectedly. But the truth is that Conan Doyle's interest in spirits started decades earlier. He began his research into the spirit world back in 1893, when he joined the Society for Psychical Research.[131] In his early days, he wasn't fully convinced that spirits were real—he just wanted to explore the possibilities. But in the last fifteen years of his life, he become a true believer. He was one of the most outspoken advocates for spiritualism in the world, and he committed himself to investigating proof of life after death. He once said that his research on spiritualism was "the most important thing in the world."[132]

All of this explains how the famous detective novelist found himself investigating a story about two teenaged girls and their fairy friends in Yorkshire in 1920. But even though he desperately wanted to believe in fairies, Conan Doyle wouldn't be taken for a fool. He needed to know for sure that these girls weren't pulling his leg. So he called in a few experts.

Conan Doyle's first step was to take the negatives of the two Cottingley fairy photographs and send them to a photography expert. The photos were mailed to the Eastman Kodak Company in London, where Conan Doyle hoped the photographers on staff would be able to tell if the image had been altered. The person assigned to the case was a man named Mr. Snelling, whom Conan Doyle says "laughs at the idea that any expert in England could deceive him with a faked photograph."[133]

"These two negatives are entirely genuine, unfaked photographs of single exposure, open-air work, show movement in the fairy figures, and there is no trace whatever of studio work involving card or paper models, dark backgrounds, painted figures, etc.," Mr. Snelling told Conan Doyle. "In my opinion they are both straight untouched pictures."[134]

With confirmation that the photos hadn't been faked, Conan Doyle set out on the second part of his mission. He needed to talk with the photographers themselves: Elsie and Frances. But he decided not to go all the way to Yorkshire himself. Instead, he called in his old friend Edward Gardner—the man who had started him down this path in the first place. And that, argues writer Mary Losure, was his first mistake.[135]

Normally, it wouldn't be a problem to send your friend on a mission to investigate the existence of fairies. But in Conan Doyle's case, the friend was already convinced that fairies were real. Before Gardner arrived, he wrote to Mrs. Wright: "I know quite well that fairies exist, and that they are very shy of showing themselves or approaching adults."[136] He explained that adults can only capture evidence of fairies with help from "friends," like Elsie and Frances—which is why it was so important that the girls take more photographs. Gardner was not the ever-rational Sherlock Holmes, who only saw the evidence in front of him. Like so many of us, he was just looking for proof of what he already believed was true.

When Gardner journeyed to the house in Cottingley, he did what he considered a thorough investigation. He first asked Mr. and Mrs. Wright for their perspective on the photos. They told him all they knew, which wasn't much: that the girls had gone out into the garden and come back with pictures of fairies. Then, Gardner asked Elsie to bring him to the spot where the pictures were taken. She led him to a small waterfall, where he questioned her extensively on the appearance and behavior of the fairies. She told him the fairies were "the palest of green, pink, mauve" and that the gnome's wings, which Gardner said looked like a moth, where actually made of musical pipes.[137]

Gardner was pretty convinced by Elsie's story. He and Conan Doyle thought of her as a simple, genuine, working-class girl—which they assumed meant she was incapable of dreaming up an elaborate hoax. But Gardner did want one more piece of evidence. He asked Elsie to take more fairy photographs as proof that she hadn't faked the originals. Elsie told Gardner that she could only speak to the fairies when Frances was around—which was a problem, because Frances was staying in Scarborough at the time. But Gardner insisted. He spoke with Frances's parents, who sent her back to Cottingley for part of her summer vacation. When Frances returned to Cottingley, the girls took two more photographs. They would be the last fairy photos the girls would ever take.[138]

THE TRUTH ABOUT FAIRIES

Gardner returned to London and reported his findings to Conan Doyle, who felt he had enough proof to share the story with the world. In 1920, he wrote a report for *The Strand Magazine*, which also published many of his Sherlock Holmes stories, about fairies frolicking through Yorkshire. And for a while, that was the end of the tale. Conan Doyle died ten years later, in 1930, believing that fairies and gnomes were real. After that, most people forgot about the Cottingley fairy photographs.

Most people, that is, except for a magician named James Randi.

James Randi, known most often by his stage name "the Amazing Randi," was an award-winning magician who won a MacArthur "genius grant" for his work on the stage. But he was also known for another passion project: investigating and debunking paranormal claims. As his 2020 obituary in the *New York Times* reports: "James Randi, a MacArthur award–winning magician ... turned his formidable savvy to investigating claims of spoon bending, mind reading, fortunetelling, ghost whispering, water dowsing, faith healing, U.F.O. spotting and sundry varieties of bamboozlement, bunco, chicanery, flimflam, flummery, humbuggery, mountebankery, pettifoggery and out-and-out quacksalvery, as he quite often saw fit to call them."[139]

In 1978, Randi turned his investigative eye to the Cottingley fairy case. For decades, no one had been able to determine how Elsie and Frances created the pictures. But Randi was certain they had been faked. He started looking more closely at the fairies themselves—and realized he'd seen them before. Back in 1915, just a few years before the photos were created, there was a children's book called *Princess Mary's Gift Book*. Princess Mary's fairies, Randi realized, looked an awful lot like Elsie and Frances's.[140]

A few years later, in 1981, the truth finally came out. In an interview with Joe Cooper for *The Unexplained* magazine, Elsie Wright confessed that she had made it all up. At sixteen, Elsie had been an aspiring artist, and it was her artistic skills that made the Cottingley fairy hoax possible. She told Cooper that she used *Princess Mary's Gift Book* as inspiration for sketches, which she then turned into paper cutouts. She held the cutouts in place with hatpins and posed them by the stream. In fact, in one picture you can see the tip of a hatpin poking through a fairy's belly—which Conan Doyle noticed, and assumed was a belly button.[141]

In a later interview with the BBC, Frances Griffiths said: "I never even thought of it being a fraud. It was just Elsie and I having a bit of fun."

She added: "People often say to me, 'Don't you feel ashamed that you have made all these poor people look like fools? They believed in you.' But I do not, because they wanted to believe."[142]

Some, like Conan Doyle, went to their graves convinced that Elsie and Frances's hoax was real. But Sir Arthur Conan Doyle knew all along that he might not be right about fairies—or any of the other wondrous things he spoke about in the last years of his life. For him, it didn't matter. The possibility of discovering something magical was worth all the time and energy he put into his investigations. He wrote near the end of his life: "We who believe in the psychic revelation ... certainly have hurled ourselves against the obstinacy of our time. Possibly we have allowed some of our lives to be gnawed away in what for the moment seemed a vain and thankless quest. Only the future can show whether the sacrifice was worth it."[143]

CHAPTER EIGHT

WHO WAS D. B. COOPER?

It was the day before Thanksgiving, November 14, 1971, when a middle-aged man in a business suit and horn-rimmed glasses walked up to the counter of Northwest Orient Airlines in Portland, Oregon, and bought himself a plane ticket to Seattle.

He called himself Dan Cooper.[144]

The man was quiet as passengers settled into their seats on Flight 305. He held a briefcase in his lap, like many other businessmen heading home for the holiday weekend. He ordered a bourbon and soda from Florence Schaffner, one of the two flight attendants on board.

Then, around 3:00 p.m., just as the plane was lifting off from the runway, Florence got out of her jump seat and went to sit beside Mr. Cooper. Her colleague, twenty-two-year-old Tina Mucklow, was confused.

"This was not the normal procedure," Tina told a reporter for *Rolling Stone* decades later.[145]

Florence motioned to Tina to pick up a note that had fallen on the floor, which the passenger had handed her moments earlier. Tina unfolded the scrap of paper, and her stomach sank.

The note read: "Miss I have a bomb here and I would like you to sit by me."[146]

On instinct, Tina reached for the phone beside her and dialed into the cockpit. She told the pilot the news: Flight 305 had been hijacked.

Then, she did the only thing she could do: she approached Dan Cooper.

"I NEED YOU TO STAY HERE"

In the aisle, Florence was busy writing down Mr. Cooper's demands on a scrap of paper. By 5:00 p.m., he wanted $200,000 in cash, two front parachutes, two back parachutes, and a fuel truck waiting on the tarmac in Seattle.

Florence took the ransom note to the cockpit, and Tina Mucklow took her colleague's place. Tina told Rolling Stone that she couldn't remember if she asked Mr. Cooper if he wanted her to sit, or if he told her, "I need you to stay here."[147] All she knew was that after she took her seat beside him, her fate was sealed. She had become Dan Cooper's messenger.

As the plane flew steadily toward Seattle, Dan Cooper opened the briefcase in his lap to show Tina Mucklow the mess of wires inside. Tina said later that it looked like sticks of dynamite hooked up to batteries. The sight of it made her sick. But instead of reaching for the barf bag, Tina started to pray. She prayed for all the passengers on board, and their families, and her cabin crew. She prayed for herself and her own family. She even prayed for the man beside her. She asked God to forgive him.

"And then I kind of let go of it," she told Rolling Stone, "I felt at peace, and I just focused on what had to be done."[148]

The flight from Portland to Seattle is short—it only takes about thirty minutes. But it took much longer than that for the FBI and police on the ground to fulfill Dan Cooper's demands. For two hours, the plane flew in circles above Puget Sound. To avoid panic, the copilot, Bill Rataczak, told passengers that they had to burn off fuel before landing because of a mechanical issue. But the reality, according to reporter Andrea Marks, was that the air traffic controllers wanted the plane to fly over water so that if the bomb did go off, hunks of decimated airplane wouldn't "rain down on the people below."[149]

When the plane finally landed, the thirty-six passengers on board Flight 305 were exchanged for the money and parachutes. Tina Mucklow took several trips off the plane to deliver the money, all in twenty-dollar bills, to Cooper. But that wasn't the end for Tina. While some crew members were set free in Seattle, Cooper kept Tina and the pilots on board. The plane refueled, and then it took off again— this time for Mexico City.[150]

THE GREAT LEAP

The plan, as far as the FBI and remaining airline crew knew, was for Cooper to fly to Mexico, with a quick stopover in Reno, Nevada, to refuel. But once the plane got off the ground, that plan changed. By that point, it was nearly 8:00 p.m., and Tina Mucklow was the only person in the cabin with Cooper. She had been sitting next to the skyjacker for more than five hours.

"I just felt so alone," she told Andrea Marks.[151]

Cooper demanded the plane stay low—he didn't want the pilots to fly over 10,000 feet, though normal cruising altitude is between 35,000 and 40,000 feet above sea level. Then, he asked Tina to take him to the stairs at the back of the airplane.

Tina opened the back door, releasing the pressure in the cabin and filling the plane with a rush of cold air. She showed Cooper how to lower the stairs, terrified the entire time that the pressure of the fast-moving plane would suck her out the door and into the stormy night.

But Cooper didn't ask Tina to stay. Instead, he told her that she could go to the cockpit with the pilots. He was preparing his parachutes. Tina knew he would jump.

Before she walked away, she remembers asking Cooper: "Will you please, please take the bomb with you?"

Copilot Bill Rataczak remembers the moment when Tina walked into the cockpit to tell them they were safe. "All of a sudden the cockpit door opened, and in walked this lovely lady who had been our passive resistance to the hijacker," he told reporters.[152]

No one on the plane checked the cabin again until they landed in Reno. When they did, they found an empty cabin—no money, no bomb, no Cooper. They were finally safe. But it wasn't until Tina and Bill were in the back of an FBI car that she finally broke down. She remembers sobbing uncontrollably, and Bill patting her on the back, soothing her. "It's okay," he said over and over. "It's okay. It's okay."[153]

But was it okay? Sure, no one got hurt—not one of the thirty-six passengers or any of the crew members. Everyone survived the skyjacking.

At least, everyone who could be accounted for.

To this day, no one knows for sure what happened to Cooper—in fact, they don't even know his real name. All agents know is that a man calling himself Dan Cooper leapt from a commercial airplane at 10,000 feet and parachuted into the forests of Oregon in a rainstorm with $200,000 in cash strapped to his chest. The case of Flight 305 remains the only unsolved skyjacking in history—and for the next five decades, the FBI would keep looking for Mr. Dan Cooper.

A MAN WITHOUT A NAME

The FBI's investigation into the identity and whereabouts of Dan Cooper began while Flight 305 was still in the air—and it didn't stop for nearly fifty years. In the early days of NORJAK, short for Northwest Hijacking, the FBI identified more than eight hundred suspects. But by the fifth anniversary of the skyjacking, only a handful of suspects remained.[154]

One suspect, Robert Rackstraw, captured the attention of author and movie producer Thomas J. Colbert, who wrote a book in 2016 arguing that all signs point to Rackstraw as the culprit. Rackstraw was a pilot and Vietnam veteran. His military background meant he had the skills to jump from a plane and survive—and two investigators in California also noted that he resembled the FBI's sketches of Dan Cooper. Colbert's website reveals that Rackstraw admitted that he was introduced to parachuting as a teenager by a beloved uncle, whose name happened to be Ed Cooper. When asked by reporters if it was legitimate that he was being considered as a suspect, he replied, "Oh yes, if I was an investigator ... I wouldn't discount myself ... or a person like myself."[155]

Most of Colbert's argument is based on coded messages found in letters from the supposed hijacker. But those messages didn't convince the FBI. In the 1980s, they ruled out Rackstraw—claiming that he wasn't old enough at the time of the skyjacking to be a legitimate suspect. Rackstraw was only twenty-seven years old in 1971—he could hardly be considered "middle-aged."

In 2018, another book came out implicating a potential suspect. Carl Laurin, who authored the book *D. B. Cooper and Me: A Criminal, A Spy, My Best Friend,* worked with reporters in Michigan to write a memoir about his friend Walter Reca, whom, for years, he suspected of being the hijacker. In 2008, Laurin collected audio recordings of his conversations with his friend Walt. In those conversations, he revealed details about the Cooper case that the FBI had never released to the public. Reca died in 2014 and was never formally charged for the crime.[156]

One favorite suspect among internet sleuths is Sheridan Peterson, a former Marine turned technical editor at Boeing. Peterson was an experienced smoke jumper, a trained firefighter who parachutes into forests to help stop wildfires before they spread. He was also known for his daring stunts, including "experimenting with homemade batwings," according to the *Spokesman-Review*.[157] Peterson died in 2021 at ninety-four years old—but while he was alive, he never denied being a suspect. In fact, he encouraged it. He once told reporters, "Actually, the FBI had good reason to suspect me … At the time of the heist, I was forty-four years old. That was the approximate age Cooper was assumed to have been, and I closely resembled sketches of the hijacker. But what was even more incriminating was the photo of me simulating a skydiving maneuver for Boeing's news sheet. I was wearing a suit and tie—the same sort of garb Cooper had worn, right down to the Oxford loafers. It was noted that skydivers don't ordinarily dress so formally."[158] Sheridan was also never charged—he wasn't even interviewed by the FBI until 2004. Friends and FBI agents remember him as a charming guy with an adventurous spirit, whose lifelong dedication to political causes more than made up for his potential involvement in this crime—if, in fact, he was Dan Cooper.

Who is the FBI's favorite suspect? There is only one person listed on their website: Richard Floyd McCoy, Jr.[159] McCoy is a favorite among amateur sleuths as well, for one reason: He got caught committing an identical crime only a few months after Cooper made his leap. On April 7, 1972, Richard Floyd McCoy, Jr. boarded United Airlines Flight 855, which was scheduled to fly from New Jersey to California. Only a few minutes after takeoff, a flight attendant noticed that McCoy was holding a hand grenade. An off-duty pilot on board was asked to investigate, and when he approached McCoy, he received a sealed envelope with typed instructions inside. The hijacker demanded four parachutes and $500,000 in cash. He told the pilots to land in San Francisco.[160]

The authorities complied with the hijacker's requests, and eventually McCoy and a stewardess acting as a messenger took off again toward Utah. McCoy then used the tools provided and a jumpsuit and helmet he had stowed in his carry-on bag and leapt from the airplane. But McCoy's plan wasn't quite as foolproof as Cooper's—namely, because he'd let someone in on his secret. McCoy, who was a Vietnam veteran, helicopter pilot, and experienced skydiver, had talked with an acquaintance about his plan. That acquaintance heard about the hijacking and immediately alerted authorities, who tracked down McCoy and took him in for questioning. Two days later, McCoy was arrested for aircraft piracy. He was eventually sentenced to forty-five years in prison.[161] The FBI never charged McCoy with the Cooper hijacking—but only because they didn't think he looked enough like their sketches.

And what about the name D. B. Cooper? Unfortunately, the initials don't reveal any hidden clues. The name came from a newspaper slipup. In the early days of the investigation, a reporter mistakenly heard someone say "D. B. Cooper" instead of "Dan Cooper"—and for some reason, the nickname stuck.

BURIED LEADS

The FBI investigated the D. B. Cooper case from 1971 until 2016, when they finally decided that they needed to focus their attention elsewhere. But in those forty-five years, they did uncover some exciting leads—including nearly $6,000 in lost ransom money and several letters signed by the hijacker himself.

First came the letters. On November 29, 1971, the *Reno Evening Gazette* received a note made from cutout newspaper clippings. It read: "Attention! Thanks for the hospitality. Was in a rut." The letter was signed, "D. B. Cooper."[162]

The newspaper forwarded the letter to the FBI, which began to investigate the source of the note. But then, more letters arrived. One letter taunted authorities, suggesting that Cooper had just left Vancouver, British Columbia, after attending the Grey Cup football game. Another said that he was alive and well, with a cryptic message: "The system that beats the system." The fifth letter, which was much longer than others, claimed that Cooper wore a toupee and putty makeup on the plane during the hijacking, and that he was alive—but only had fourteen months to live. "I'm no modern day Robin Hood," the letter says, "this seemed to be the fastest and most profitable way to gain a few fast grains of peace of mind."[163]

The sixth and final letter was also taunting, calling police "silly troopers" and claiming that Cooper had just returned from a vacation in the Bahamas. It ended, "Please tell the lackey cops D. B. Cooper is not my real name."[164]

Eventually, Thomas J. Colbert would use these letters to try to decipher the real identity of Cooper, leading him to suspect (and write a whole book about) Robert Rackstraw. But the FBI didn't buy it. They assumed the letters were all a hoax, though they did hold on to two of them until 2000. Some experts assume that means they had their doubts.[165] But the letters didn't lead investigators anywhere—at least, not to the identity of Dan Cooper.

Then, in 1980, there was a major break in the case. A boy digging on the banks of the Columbia River near Vancouver, Washington, found a pile of twenty-dollar bills—and their serial numbers matched Cooper's ransom money. All told, the treasure amounted to $5,800. Immediately, investigators began searching, hoping to find more money, or even the remains of Cooper's body.[166]

But the FBI found nothing. No money, no briefcase, no Cooper. That lead went cold. At least until a crime historian decided to resurrect it.

In August 2021, D. B. Cooper expert Eric Ulis decided to dig. He claimed that the FBI didn't thoroughly investigate the banks of the Columbia, because they didn't properly trace the flight path of the hijacked airplane. "Simply put, the authorities were looking in the wrong area," says Ulis.[167] Ulis and a team of volunteers planned to dig near the site where the ransom money was found, in search of the briefcase and parachutes that Cooper likely left behind.

Ulis's search was livestreamed on Facebook. He and four volunteers dug out eight to ten square feet of riverbank—but they didn't find anything.

"After two days of digging we managed to basically dig down through a very difficult layer of rock that was placed upon the beach several years back to stop erosion," Ulis said on the D. B. Cooper Mystery Group private Facebook page after the event. "We now have a solid idea of the strata layout on this very important part of Tena Bar ... The plan now needs to be to dig down another 18 inches into the beach to see what we find."

"Needless to say this will take some time," he adds.

Ulis planned on continuing his dig in November 2021. Until he finds more, what's buried under decades of rock and sand remains a mystery.

A LOCAL LEGEND

At the Ariel General Store and Tavern in Ariel, Washington, there is a crowd of people wearing the same outfit—black suit, white shirt, black tie, black sunglasses.

But this isn't a business conference. It's D. B. Cooper Day.[168]

Every year, people gather in Ariel to compete over who looks the most like the FBI sketches of the only skyjacker ever to get away with his crime. There's live music and food—it's a happy celebration. And it's not the only event where Cooper is the star. In the Pacific Northwest, where Cooper is still a local legend, there are music festivals, restaurants, bars, and annual costume contests named after the infamous criminal. Eric Ulis even hosts an annual CooperCon to discuss the legendary crime, which includes an "air tour" of his suspected landing zone on the Columbia River.

But why do people still care about a fifty-year-old crime?

For some people, Cooper is an unlikely, romantic hero—a Robin Hood who committed a nonviolent crime and absconded with a whole lot of money, never to be seen again. For others, the case is proof that the perfect crime is possible. D. B. Cooper stole a commercial airplane and managed to get away with it.

But for Tina Mucklow, Dan Cooper wasn't a Robin Hood—or a romantic hero. He was real man, who threatened her life. "[Dan Cooper] was a criminal," Mucklow told *Rolling Stone*, when asked how she felt about the FBI ending their investigation of the case. "Who was not only threatening my life, but the lives of all those innocent people on that flight."[169]

Tina continued to work as a flight attendant for ten years after the hijacking, and then she left her profession to become a Catholic nun. Later, she went to school to be a social worker, where she focused her attention on helping others. She has staffed mental health crisis lines and worked with homeless populations in Eugene, Oregon, where she lives.

The real and often forgotten hero of this story is Tina.

"I was a crew member who was just trying to do my job to the best of my ability, along with my fellow crew members, and if we had an agenda, it was to get that airplane safely on the ground and the passengers off the airplane," Tina told Andrea Marks. "I think that's probably what all of us would want to be remembered for."[170]

CHAPTER NINE

THE PHOENIX LIGHTS

On Thursday, March 13, 1997, a fifty-one-year-old cement truck driver named Bill Grenier was driving down the side of a mountain outside Phoenix, Arizona, when something in the night sky caught his eye. It was bright, and orb-like. He blinked a few times and shook his head. He looked again. In the sky far above him were two glimmering objects. They looked, he told reporters later, like spinning tops.[171]

Meanwhile, across the state of Arizona, phones were ringing. The first phone call came in around 8:15 p.m. A retired police officer living in Paulden, about sixty miles north of Phoenix, rang the police. He saw something, he told the dispatcher. A cluster of five brilliant red lights floated past his house, heading south.

Two minutes later, another call. Fifteen miles south of Paulden, in Prescott, a bystander watched four white lights and one red one zoom by, heading toward Phoenix.

The phones rang and rang—at police stations, at newspapers, at Luke Air Force Base. And every single caller was saying the same thing. There was something in the sky above Arizona. And it looked like it came from another world.[172]

SIGHTINGS

It started as a normal Thursday evening for Tim Ley, his son Hal, and his wife Bobbi. Tim, a managing consultant, hopped out of his truck around 8:00 p.m. He was just getting home from work. But when he stepped out of the cab, his jaw dropped. Above him, a shadow was hovering in the sky. It was enormous, bigger than anything he'd ever seen.

Ley grabbed his wife and son, and the family stepped out onto the lawn to watch the object pass over their heads.

Ley, and hundreds of other witnesses who saw the object that night, later reported that it was the size of three football fields, or perhaps even larger. Supposedly, it was V-shaped, though many witnesses said it was hard to determine its real shape and size because it wasn't lit up.

"It was so big and so strange," said Tim Ley. "You couldn't actually see the object. All you could see was the outline, as though something was blotting out the stars."[173]

Dana Valentine and his father, who were also Phoenix residents at the time, stood open-mouthed as the object drifted slowly over their heads, about five hundred feet in the air.

"We could see the outline of a mass behind the lights," Valentine said. "But you couldn't actually see the mass. It was more like a gray distortion of the night sky, wavy."[174]

"It didn't seem threatening," Bobbi Ley told reporters after the event. "When it was right overhead and we couldn't hear a sound, it was like you're just awestruck."[175]

Hundreds of people saw this V-shaped object drift over Phoenix that night—including doctors, lawyers, celebrities, and an entire Little League team and their families. But that wasn't the only peculiar sighting that Thursday night. Witnesses also saw a collection of glowing red and white orbs in the skyline. Unlike the V-shaped object, these lights were stationary. They hung in the sky for a few hours before disappearing into the desert night.

Later, reporters would call these two distinct sightings the "Phoenix Lights"—though what produced those lights has long been up for debate. When the government refused to investigate these occurrences, the conversation soon veered toward the extraterrestrial. After all, it wasn't the first time that something otherworldly had appeared in the American Southwest.

A CRASH LANDING IN ROSWELL

Fifty years before lights appeared in the night sky above Phoenix, locals made another extraterrestrial discovery. On June 14, 1947, Mac Brazel, a rancher outside Roswell, New Mexico, woke up to find the remnants of a mysterious-looking object in his pasture. The field was full of metal poles stuck together with tape, foil reflectors, and a strange paper-like material that was heavy and glossy.[176]

To the untrained eye, the debris looked like the remnants of a spaceship.

Brazel immediately called the sheriff, who in turn called the nearby Roswell Army Air Field. Soldiers promptly arrived to cart off the debris, piling the metallic sticks and foil into the back of armored trucks. The military claimed that the mess was created by a weather balloon. But Brazel, and many other local residents, weren't so sure. There were rumors flying around town that in the remains of the foil and glossy paper, there was a body. And it didn't look human.[177]

Since that day in 1947, millions of tourists have trekked to Roswell, New Mexico, to see the supposed location of the unidentified flying object (UFO). But tourists weren't the only people investigating the possibility of life on other planets. The Air Force had some questions of their own after the Roswell incident. To answer those questions, they launched a new initiative: Project Blue Book.[178]

Project Blue Book was an ongoing Air Force investigation that lasted from 1947, just after the Roswell incident, to 1969. The purpose of the project was simple: to investigate the possible presence of UFOs. During the two decades that Project Blue Book was active, the Air Force received 12,618 reports of UFO sightings from across the nation. Of those more than 12,000 reports, 701 of the incidents have never been explained. However, in 1985 the Wright-Patterson Air Force Base, which was the headquarters for this project, released a fact sheet on the project. In that document, they claim that the Air Force never found evidence that any UFO had otherworldly origins. They wrote:

> [T]he conclusions of Project BLUE BOOK are: (1) no UFO reported, investigated, and evaluated by the Air Force has ever given any indication of threat to our national security; (2) there has been no evidence submitted to or discovered by the Air Force that sightings categorized as "unidentified" represent technological developments or principles beyond the range of present-day scientific knowledge; and (3) there has been no evidence indicating that sightings categorized as "unidentified" are extraterrestrial vehicles.[179]

But if the Air Force found no proof of extraterrestrials, what happened on that ranch in Roswell? As it turns out, the Army knew more than they were willing to admit. During World War II, the military was experimenting with high-altitude balloons, which they wired with audio equipment and launched high into the atmosphere. This distant part of the atmosphere, also called the troposphere, can act as a sound channel—meaning that noise can travel for thousands of miles. The government hoped that by launching these high-altitude balloons, they would be able to hear nuclear testing in the Soviet Union and gather valuable intelligence.[180] The debris that landed in Brazel's field was likely one of these balloons.

DEBUNKED

Project Blue Book ended in 1969—nearly three decades before the Phoenix Lights appeared in the desert sky. So when those lights appeared, the government had no interest in investigating. As they write in their report: "Since Project BLUE BOOK was closed, nothing has happened to indicate that the Air Force ought to resume investigating UFOs. Because of the considerable cost to the Air Force in the past, and the tight funding of Air Force needs today, there is no likelihood the Air Force will become involved with UFO investigation again."[181]

But the lack of investigation angered locals. They knew what they had seen, and they weren't backing down. Bill Grenier, the cement truck driver, claims that the night he saw the Phoenix Lights, he was driving about a mile from the Luke Air Force Base. He says he saw one of the orbs lingering over the base, and watched three F-16 jets take off and approach the orb. But as soon as they got close, the orb shot straight into the sky and disappeared.[182]

"I'll take a lie detector test on national TV if that guy from the base does the same thing," Grenier told reporters a few months later. "I wish the government would just admit it. It's like having 50,000 people in a stadium watch a football game and then having someone tell us we weren't there."[183]

Without any help from local officials, reporters and other amateur sleuths had to take the investigation into their own hands. And they did just that. According to the *Phoenix New Times*, a young man named Mitch Stanley in Scottsdale, Arizona, looked at the Phoenix Lights through a telescope and clearly saw pairs of wings attached to each light.

"Even under the telescope's power, the planes appeared small, indicating that they were flying high." Stanley says he followed the planes for about a minute, then turned his telescope to more interesting objects. "They were planes. There's no way I could have mistaken that," he says.[184]

The report adds that the strange V-shaped object was likely several planes flying in formation.

"Some people thought all the lights were part of one craft," reporter Matthew Hendley writes, "but an analysis of the videotape made it clear that they were moving together in a formation, but they were independent of one another."[185]

Unfortunately, no one thought to check the radar information from the Federal Aviation Administration for that night. The records are deleted every two weeks—so the truth behind that V-shaped shadow may never be known for sure.

A SECOND VISIT

For ten years, the skies above Phoenix were quiet. And then, on April 21, 2008, residents looked out their windows to see a familiar sight.

High above the city, there were four glowing red orbs.[186]

Residents watched as the pattern of the orbs slowly changed, moving from a triangular to a rectangular configuration. Then, slowly, they disappeared, blinking out one by one.

The phones rang again at police stations and newspapers across the county. The Air Force had no explanation, and neither did air traffic controllers in the area.

But for those who still believed, the answer was simple: the aliens were back for a second visit.

Unlike the incident in 1997, it only took two days for this second mystery to reveal itself. On April 23, a local news station aired breaking news. There had been a confession.

As it turns out, an anonymous hoaxer was behind the whole escapade—including the 1997 incident. He claimed that two nights earlier, he had tied road flares to four helium balloons and launched them one minute apart. The balloons drifted into the air and then eventually popped.[187]

There's no proof that the orbs were in fact the work of a con artist. But writer Benjamin Radford believes that the story is likely true—or at least, more likely than an alien invasion. Radford explains that helium balloons tied with fishing line would be invisible on air traffic control radar, while a spaceship would not. He also reported that the pattern of the objects matches the way balloons move in air currents.

"The mysterious lights drifted toward the east," he writes, "in the same direction as the wind."[188]

TRUE BELIEVERS

Though reporters have gotten to the bottom of the Phoenix Lights mystery, there are still people who believe that what they saw the night of March 13, 1997, was from another world. Bill Grenier is one of them. And so is former Arizona governor Fife Symington, who was serving his second term in office when the Phoenix Lights appeared on the horizon. In an article on the CNN website in 2007, Symington said:

> In 1997, during my second term as governor of Arizona, I saw something that defied logic and challenged my reality.
>
> I witnessed a massive delta-shaped, craft silently navigate over Squaw Peak, a mountain range in Phoenix, Arizona. It was truly breathtaking. I was absolutely stunned because

I was turning to the west looking for the distant Phoenix Lights.

To my astonishment this apparition appeared; this dramatically large, very distinctive leading edge with some enormous lights was traveling through the Arizona sky.

As a pilot and a former Air Force Officer, I can definitively say that this craft did not resemble any man-made object I'd ever seen.[189]

For many people, the Phoenix Lights were a life-changing experience, and one that can't easily be explained away. Though the military and other investigators have offered explanations, for these people, the events of March 13, 1997, will forever be proof that someone, or something, is out there. As Symington says: "There might very well have been military flares in the sky that evening, but what I and hundreds of others saw had nothing to do with that."[190]

We may not ever know the true stories behind the thousands of UFO sightings that are reported across the world each year. But for the US government, at least, the investigation isn't over. In 2021, the Pentagon announced that they are forming a new task force called the Airborne Object Identification and Management Synchronization Group. This group will investigate reports of UFO sightings near sensitive military areas to determine whether they are actual security risks, or just hearsay. Who knows, in the years to come, what mysteries they'll uncover.[191]

CHAPTER TEN

FOOTPRINTS IN THE SAND

There wasn't much going on in Clearwater, Florida, in 1948. There were only about fifteen thousand residents and a small population of tourists that showed up every winter to sunbathe on Clearwater's white, sandy beaches. It was a sleepy suburb—that is, until one February morning, when the police received a phone call from a local resident. He was frantic.

It appeared, he said, that Clearwater, Florida, had been visited by a monster.[192]

The man on the phone refused to give his name. He had been parked on the beach with a girl, he explained, and he didn't want to get anyone in trouble. But in the early hours of the morning, he'd seen something strange. A creature had emerged from the ocean and started wandering Clearwater Beach.

The man on the phone then asked the chief of police if he could borrow a rifle and take care of the problem once and for all.[193]

The police didn't give the man a gun. But they did drive over to Clearwater Beach to check out the evidence. In the sand were dozens of enormous, three-toed footprints. The prints were about fourteen inches long and eleven inches wide. The stride was more than four feet long, and the prints sunk almost an inch into the sand. The prints emerged from the sea and returned to the water a few yards later.

The police chief had never seen anything like it.[194]

Clearwater residents flocked to the beach, curious to get a glimpse of the prints themselves. Some people wondered if a massive crocodile from the salt marsh nearby had somehow found its way to the ocean. Some speculated it might be a bear. Others wondered if it was one of the famous sea turtles that lay their eggs on Clearwater Beach each winter.

But the police chief didn't buy any of those answers. "If it was a sea turtle," he said, "it was the granddaddy of them all."[195]

As residents pondered what kind of animal could be responsible for the mysterious prints in the sand, the police got another call.

The monster was at it again.

A MONSTER AFOOT

The police rushed to Indian Rocks Bridge, about six miles away. It was 11:00 p.m., and pitch-black. When the police arrived, the monster was nowhere to be seen—but a local woman said that she knew the creature had been roaming. Only a half hour before, her dog had started howling and barking at the water's edge.

Upon further investigation, the police found more three-toed prints.[196]

That certainly wasn't the last sighting of the infamous Clearwater Monster. One couple claimed they saw an enormous, hairy creature waddling on the beach, which then disappeared into the ocean. A group of students at the local Dunedin Flying Club saw a massive, unidentifiable animal swimming under the Clearwater Memorial Causeway Bridge.[197] And footprints kept showing up everywhere— on the Sarasota waterfront, on the beach by the Courtney Campbell Causeway. The animal was making its rounds along the entire Pinellas Peninsula.[198]

The media went wild, and reporters flocked to the beaches looking for the next break in the Clearwater Monster story. And those headlines drew the attention of one man in particular—a charming zoologist named Ivan T. Sanderson, who had a passion for mythical beasts.

THE SOCIETY FOR THE INVESTIGATION OF THE UNEXPLAINED

Ivan T. Sanderson was born in Scotland in 1911. As an adult, he became a world traveler, radio reporter, and self-taught zoologist. He was particularly interested in rare animals—and was known for showing off those creatures in his home, on TV, and on radio talk shows.[199] Many people claim that he used to enjoy walking into five-star restaurants with a parrot on his shoulder.[200]

Sanderson started collecting animals in 1924, when he was at Eton College. He went on to travel and collect specimens for the British Museum in the late 1920s, and he led expeditions to West Africa and beyond, gathering creatures for the Royal Society of London and other institutions. In the 1930s, Sanderson traveled on his own, collecting animal specimens and reporting on his findings in books and on the radio.

In the 1950s, after serving in World War II as part of the British Naval Intelligence Division, Sanderson moved to the United States. He soon became popular on TV as a naturalist with a passion for the rarest and strangest creatures on the planet. In fact, some of the creatures were so strange, no one was quite sure they were real. Around this time, Sanderson invented the word "cryptozoology" to describe his passion project—studying animals from myth and local folklore that no one had been able to capture before.[201] He even started a scientific community dedicated to uncovering the secrets of these beasts. He called it the Society for the Investigation of the Unexplained.

Sanderson became famous for his study of creatures like the Abominable Snowman, the Loch Ness Monster, and Bigfoot—though the Society for the Investigation of the Unexplained also covered unsolved mysteries in astronomy, geology, chemistry, and more.[202] He wrote books on these mythical creatures, with photos from his travels to illustrate his findings. And it was his interest in cryptozoology that brought Sanderson to Clearwater, Florida. He was determined to uncover the identity of the creature behind those three-toed prints.

Sanderson started his investigation with the best piece of evidence he had—the footprints themselves. He used plaster to make a cast of the three-toed feet. After careful examination of the prints, Sanderson determined that they absolutely could not have been man-made. The curvature of one of the toes proved that.[203]

Sanderson drew some other conclusions, too. He believed the creature was likely "pudgy," based on the size, shape, and depth of the footprint. He also said the creature seemed sad—or perhaps lost. He appeared to be wandering aimlessly on the beach, as if he were looking for someone.

Sanderson spent a few days investigating, including trips in a small biplane over the peninsula looking for signs of the beast. He didn't find anything. In the end, he used the only evidence he had—the footprints—to come up with an answer. The Clearwater Monster was a giant penguin.[204] The bird, he said, could be up to fifteen feet tall.

Interestingly, Sanderson wasn't totally off base with his penguin suggestion—though he couldn't have known it at the time. In recent years, scientists have uncovered dozens of skeletons of giant penguins, which lived thirty to sixty-million years ago in New Zealand and South America. But thus far, the largest of these birds was about five feet, three inches tall, and about 176 pounds.[205] Those real ancient penguins would be dwarfed by Sanderson's giant bird.

Some Clearwater residents were convinced by Sanderson's testimony—others remained skeptical. But for one family in town, the identity of the monster was not a mystery at all. They even had their own name for him.

They called him Tony.

MEET TONY

Tony Signorini was born and raised in Monongahela, Pennsylvania, where he married his high school sweetheart, Elsie.[206] During World War II, Tony worked in the Army Air Corps as a flight engineer. At the end of the war, Elsie and Tony decided to celebrate with a vacation in Florida. They spent two weeks in Clearwater, and at the end of their stay both seemed hesitant to go home. As Jeff Signorini, their son, tells it, Elise reluctantly suggested they pack their suitcases, and Tony asked her "Why?" He wasn't going anywhere. The couple moved to Clearwater and never looked back.

In Clearwater, Tony and Elsie became active members of St. Cecelia Catholic Church. Tony got a job as a mechanic, where he worked alongside a man named Al Williams. Al was known for being a bit of a grouch. Jeff Signorini calls him a "curmudgeon" in his interview with Phoebe Judge.[207] But Tony saw something in Al that others didn't see. He thought Al was hilarious. Al loved to play practical jokes—and as it turns out, so did Tony.

Al and Tony became notorious around town for their pranks. Because they were both mechanics, many of their pranks revolved around cars. They liked to put whistles in their friends' ignition switches, so the cars would make strange, high-pitched noises when they turned the key. On Saturday nights, when most of Clearwater gathered at a local dance, the men would wander through the parking lot and swap out car hoods. When the dancers came out, it was too dark to notice—but the next morning, they'd wake up to find that their green car had a red hood.

Once, Jeff says, Al and Tony managed to sneak a horse into the holding cell at the police station. They locked him in as a surprise for the officers in the morning.[208] To this day, no one knows how they did it.

So, it wasn't out of character when Al showed Tony a *National Geographic* photo spread. The pictures were of preserved dinosaur footprints.

"We could really do something with this," Al said.

A few weeks later, Tony got a new identity. He would now appear in newspaper headlines across the nation as the Clearwater Monster.

MAKING A MONSTER

To become the Clearwater Monster, Tony didn't need an elaborate costume. He just needed some sneakers. Really big sneakers.

Al and Tony used the *National Geographic* photo to sketch out a model of a realistic-looking monster foot. Using that sketch, they made a plaster cast and then used cement to make two matching dinosaur feet. Then, they strapped the cement feet onto a pair of Converse and headed to the beach in the dead of night.[209]

But the cement feet weren't as convincing as Al hoped. They weren't heavy enough to leave a deep imprint in the sand—and Al and Tony knew that a real monster would weigh enough to leave a proper print. So the men went back to the drawing board, this time with the help of another friend in town. This friend was a metal worker, and he used the cast to make two cast-iron dinosaur feet for Al and Tony. When strapped to the Converse sneakers, these metal feet weighed almost 30 pounds.[210] It was finally time for Tony to make his debut.

The men went to Clearwater Beach in the middle of the night— back then, the shoreline was mostly undeveloped, and there were few lights to reveal their scheme. They took a small boat out into the ocean, and then Al rowed Tony close to shore. Tony, wearing the monster feet, hopped out of the boat and began his roaming trek out onto the sand. But he wasn't just going for a quick walk. To get the stride right, he would plant one foot in the sand and then swing his other leg as far out as it would go. Using this method, he was able to get a stride of between four and six feet—much more monstrous than his normal gait.

Once Tony was done clomping around on the shore, Al would meet him in the boat again, and Tony would trek back into the sea and climb in. Then, they would row home, giggling all the way.

That first night, Tony came back home around 2:00 a.m. When Elsie came down to meet him, he was covered in sand and couldn't stop laughing. He couldn't wait to tell her what he and Al had done.[211]

For the next forty years, Al and Tony watched as the myth of the Clearwater Monster swept the state—and the nation. They watched as Ivan T. Sanderson arrived, with his slicked-back hair and dainty mustache, to investigate the prints. They read about all the supposed sightings. And occasionally, when they felt like it had been a while since the last Clearwater Monster headline, they would whip out the monster feet and bring the creature back to life.

Then, in 1970, Al Williams died. Tony and his family were the only people left keeping the mystery alive. Eventually, in 1988, Tony decided it was time to reveal the truth. He invited a reporter to his workshop, where he had stored the monster shoes in a pile under his desk for the last few decades.

"Clearwater can relax," the headline read the next morning. "Monster unmasked."[212]

SEEING IS BELIEVING

When Tony Signorini died in 2012 at ninety-one years of age, his obituary talked about his lifelong marriage to his high school sweetheart. It mentioned his commitment to his church and his military service. And it also named him as the Clearwater Monster.

"Tony was famous for being the 'Clearwater Monster,'" the obituary reads, "a hoax that made national news during the late 40's and 50's and remained unsolved for decades."[213]

His son, Jeff, who wrote that obituary, told reporter Phoebe Judge that it would have been wrong not to mention his dad's greatest prank.

"It was something he took great joy in," Jeff said. "It was part of him."[214]

But Tony and Al did more than just pull off a great prank. They brought a creature to life—and gave people the opportunity to imagine a wilder, more mysterious world.

"A lot of mystery has just disappeared," says Jeff Signorini. "It's funny when something can knock us for a loop. It gives you a sense of wonder."[215]

The Clearwater Monster might not have been a fifteen-foot-tall penguin or a hairy beast emerging from the sea. But it was real, because Al and Tony made it real. They created a world in which the Clearwater Monster might exist. They allowed the people of Clearwater to believe, at least for a little while, that a monster can simply appear one day and wander the shores of your hometown.

For a few decades, in Clearwater, Florida, anything was possible.

CHAPTER ELEVEN

SEEING LINCOLN'S GHOST

On a balmy spring day in April 1869, court was in session in New York City. But it wasn't a thief or a murderer on trial. It was a middle-aged man named William H. Mumler.[216]

His crime? Taking pictures of ghosts.

For years, Mumler made a living taking "spirit photographs" out of his studio in Boston, Massachusetts. Customers were amazed by his work. Mumler claimed he could channel the spirits of your long-departed loved ones—and then capture them forever on film.

But in April 1869, Mumler wasn't channeling any spirits. He was defending his honor—and his craft. Before the trial was over, Mumler would have to contend with one of the toughest skeptics of all time. A man who made his own living fooling "suckers."[217] A man named P. T. Barnum.

A SPIRIT APPEARS

Mumler's story begins in Boston in the early 1860s. Back then, Mumler was a jewelry engraver, but he was also fascinated by photography. He didn't know then that his hobby would land him in the famous Tombs prison.

Mumler had a small photography studio that he visited on the weekends with a glass-plate camera, some props, and a dark room where he processed his pictures. Photographs were a brand-new invention back then—they had only been around for about twenty years. At the time, cameras were large and expensive, and most people would visit professional photographers to get their picture taken. Mumler had some money to spare, so he decided to dabble in this new technology, which married science and art.

One Sunday afternoon, Mumler was tinkering with his camera when he decided to try taking a self-portrait. He set up the camera the same way he always did and stood in front of the lens. When the shutter clicked and the photo was taken, Mumler hurried the plate into the darkroom to see what he'd made. But when he dipped the picture in the solution and an image slowly appeared, he was shocked. In the foreground, Mumler saw his own face. But beside him, there was the outline of a little girl sitting in a chair. She was so pale she was transparent.

She looked, Mumler thought, like a ghost.[218]

At first, Mumler didn't think anything more of it. He was just an amateur after all. He assumed he'd accidentally taken two photos on the same plate, called a "double exposure," which made it look like the ghost girl was beside him. But the image was so spooky, Mumler couldn't help but show a few friends. One of those friends was a man named Dr. H. F. Gardner.

Gardner was a spiritualist, which means he believed that ghosts can communicate with the living. Gardner was immediately drawn to the picture, and he started asking Mumler questions. He believed that the girl in the photo really was a spirit. He also believed that Mumler had channeled her. The more he talked, the more intrigued Mumler became. By the end of the conversation, Mumler was a believer—and he had an idea for a new business.[219]

CAPTURING THE INVISIBLE

Somehow, Mumler's photos ended up in a spiritualist newspaper as proof that ghosts could interact with the living on film. At first, Mumler was "considerably mortified."[220] But when people started calling him, asking to have their photo taken, he agreed. The first few pictures didn't produce much. But then, spirits started appearing in the background of his shots. When spirits did appear, the visitors were grateful. Photographs were expensive, and most people didn't have any pictures of themselves or their families. For some people, Mumler's photo, with its strange white shadow of their ghostly relative, was the only picture they had of their dead son, daughter, brother, or friend.

After those few sittings were a success, Mumler decided he would go into business. He started taking pictures for two hours every day. Any more, he claimed, would drain his "spiritual energy." Without that, ghosts wouldn't appear.[221]

Today, we probably wouldn't believe a man who claims he can take pictures of ghosts. But for most people in the 1800s, photography was still new, and it seemed magical. "Photography could capture the living, but there was also this idea that photography could capture the invisible,"[222] says Louis Kaplan, author of the book *The Strange Case of William Mumler, Spirit Photographer*. At the time, the Civil War was going on, and young men were dying by the thousands on the battlefields. People wanted to believe that they could see their sons one last time—and Mumler and his magical art of spirit photography made them believe that was possible.

When a visitor came to Mumler's studio, they would be greeted by Hannah Mumler, William's wife. Hannah was friendly and kind. She made people feel comfortable—and she also asked them questions. Hannah would determine why a visitor had come and whom they lost. She also claimed to be a medium, and she often sat in on sessions to reassure customers that their dearly departed loved ones would appear.

Once Hannah greeted the customer, they would head into the studio. Inside, William Mumler stood behind his camera. He would help visitors pose so they would look nice in the photo, sometimes offering them props like instruments or flowers. Mumler would take the picture, and then the family would wait with bated breath to see if a spirit appeared.[223]

The most unique thing about Mumler's pictures wasn't just that he could capture ghosts, but that the ghosts would interact with the sitters. A ghost might hold out a bouquet of flowers to their family member, or be captured lowering a wreath onto their loved one's head. Children were often shown sitting on their parents' laps. One of Mumler's pictures shows a ghost plucking the strings on her family member's guitar.[224] Because the pictures were interactive, customers believed they couldn't possibly be faked. Plus, many of Mumler's customers recognized their family members. How could you argue with that?

By the end of the 1860s, Mumler was making his living from his spirit photographs. He had dozens of happy customers—but then, things started to slip. Other photographers started to get suspicious when so-called "ghosts" would appear in Mumler's photographs that were not, in fact, dead at all.

For Mumler, it was the beginning of the end.

GHOSTS AND CIRCUSES

The first suspicious photograph Mumler took was of a missing soldier. A woman came into Mumler's studio asking for a picture with her brother, who hadn't come home from the Civil War. The photo shoot was a success. The woman went home with a portrait of her brother's ghost standing beside her. She was a happy customer— or so Mumler thought.

The trouble didn't start until a few weeks later, when the woman opened her front door to discover her brother on her doorstep. He was home from the war.

It appeared, she said, that Mumler had channeled the spirit of a ghost who didn't yet exist.[225]

The second suspicious photo was even more alarming. A man came into Mumler's studio asking for a portrait. When Mumler processed the photo, the ghost of the man's wife appeared beside him. But the man wasn't happy with the results. His wife, he informed Mumler, was very much alive. In fact, she'd sat for a portrait with Mumler just a few months before. In this new picture, her ghost was even wearing the same hat.[226]

These two incidents alarmed local photographers and customers, who started to wonder whether Mumler had supernatural abilities or was just a master of persuasion. Mumler could tell that people were getting wary of him, and he decided it was time to leave Boston and relocate to New York. But his problems seemed to follow him. One disgruntled customer called the mayor, claiming that Mumler was committing fraud. The mayor was interested in the potential scam. But to prove Mumler was a fake, they needed evidence—and the best person to gather that evidence was a New York marshal named Joseph Tooker.[227]

Tooker decided that the best way to prove that Mumler was a phony was to catch him in the act. So one afternoon, he walked into the famous studio and requested a sitting. As usual, Hannah Mumler started asking questions. Tooker told her that he was trying to get in touch with the spirit of his dead father-in-law. Mumler ushered Tooker into the studio and sat him down in front of the camera. A few days later, when Tooker came back to the studio to pick up the portrait, Mumler was pleased. The photo showed Tooker next to the shadowy figure of an older man. But Tooker shook his head. He told Mumler he didn't recognize the person in the photo—it was a fake. Then he arrested Mumler for false claims, fraud, and larceny.[228]

Mumler spent a few weeks in the famous Tombs prison in Manhattan before his trial began in April. Meanwhile, the newspapers were going wild. It wasn't just a photographer on the stand. Spiritualism itself was on trial. The people of America wanted to know: Can you really speak with ghosts?

In the courtroom, there were two groups: the people who believed in Mumler's unique ability to channel spirits and the people who believed he was a fake. The defense called up dozens of happy customers, including many prominent members of society. A Wall Street banker and a former judge both defended Mumler, and so did a handful of famous photographers who claimed that they had gone into Mumler's studio themselves to try to figure out how he did it. According to court transcripts, none of them could find anything suspicious about his process.

On the other side of the courtroom were other photographers. These experts claimed that they could also create so-called "spirit photographs"—but they weren't channeling ghosts. It was all in the technique. The most memorable witness for the prosecution, however, wasn't a photographer at all. He was a showman himself— and the owner of a local museum. His name was P. T. Barnum.[229]

You may know P. T. Barnum as the king of circuses. The famous Barnum and Bailey circus started in 1871 and was eventually sold to the Ringling Brothers, who ran the traveling show until 2017. But before he brought circuses to America, P. T. Barnum was famous for another kind of attraction, which he called Barnum's American Museum.[230]

The American Museum ran from 1841 to 1865. Located in Manhattan, the massive museum was famous for its rotating exhibits, which included oddities like the Fiji mermaid (which was actually the skeleton of a monkey sewn onto the body of a fish) and performer General Tom Thumb,[231] who had dwarfism and was only about three feet tall.

Barnum also had some photos in his museum from Mumler's studio. The label next to them read "bogus spirit photographs."

Barnum wasn't opposed to a good old-fashioned hoax. He'd made his living off them, after all. But he was opposed to Mumler acting like he could channel the supernatural. For Barnum, getting involved in matters of the afterlife was taking a good prank too far. So Barnum decided to take matters into his own hands and conduct an investigation of his own. To prove that Mumler was a fraud, Barnum paid another experienced photographer to capture his portrait with the ghost of President Abraham Lincoln. In court, Barnum held up the portrait for the audience to see. It showed the famous businessman with the ghostly, but very much recognizable, face of the late president. It was proof, he thought, that Mumler was a fake.[232]

But, even with Barnum's shocking revelation, there was one problem. No one could explain how Mumler did it.

The prosecution had a few ideas about how Mumler created his pictures. They thought he might pay an actor dressed in white makeup to sneak into the room during sessions. They also suspected Mumler might print the ghostly images onto the paper before processing the photos. But the most likely explanation, said the prosecution, was that Mumler had many different techniques, which he would use depending on how closely he was being watched.

Meanwhile, Mumler was adamant that he was innocent. "I positively assert," he said in the trial, "that in taking the pictures, I have never used any trick or device."[233]

At the end of the trial, the judge declared his verdict: Mumler was innocent. But even the judge wasn't happy about his decision. He told the court that he was frustrated he couldn't convict the photographer, because he was clearly a fraudster. But the fact of the matter was that they didn't know how Mumler was doing it—and that meant that at the end of the day, they couldn't prove the ghostly photos weren't real.

SEEING LINCOLN'S GHOST

After the trial, Mumler was a free man. He returned to his studio, where he kept taking pictures—though he no longer claimed to channel ghosts. And then one day in 1872, the ghost of Abraham Lincoln returned to haunt Mumler again.

It was a regular day for Mumler when an elegant-looking woman walked through the door. She was dressed entirely in black, with a black veil covering her face. She was clearly deep in mourning. The woman said that she had recently lost her son and would like to try to connect with his spirit one last time.

Mumler did what he always did with his visitors: He made them comfortable in the studio in front of his famous camera. But when the woman finally lifted her black veil for the portrait, Mumler was shocked. In front of him was Mary Todd Lincoln, the former first lady and the wife of Honest Abe.[234]

It was well known that Mary Lincoln's son Tad had died the year earlier of tuberculosis at only eighteen years of age. Mumler, to his credit, didn't bat an eye. He snapped a picture of the first lady, the way he would with any other customer. But when he processed the photo, it wasn't only her son Tad who appeared. The ghost of Abe Lincoln was there too, standing beside his wife. His hands rested gently on her shoulders.[235]

CHAPTER TWELVE

THE WOMAN WITH ALL THE NUMBERS

At 409 Edgecombe Avenue in Harlem, New York, a Black woman in a colorful turban and a long, dramatic fur coat breezes into the building. She wears a pearl necklace and short, fashionable heels that tip-tap as she walks across the lobby. People turn as she passes by. They know her, after all. Everyone knows her. She is Stephanie St. Clair: the woman with the numbers.

For the few years she was in the spotlight, Stephanie St. Clair made a name for herself in Harlem. She was a gangster, a businesswoman, and a fashion icon. She had money—lots of it—and she used it to support Black businesses and Caribbean immigrants like herself, who were struggling to make it in America. She single-handedly fought off a white mobster who was wreaking havoc in her neighborhood. And she was committed to racial justice. As she wrote in one of the many newspaper ads she took out during the height of her fame: "I am going to continue to fight until the members of my race get their just and legal rights."[236]

But Stephanie St. Clair wasn't born with money. Her success was all about luck—in that it started with a game of chance. The game was called policy, bolita, or the Italian lottery—in Harlem, St. Clair called it "numbers."

PLAYING THE NUMBERS

In the US in the 1930s, it was virtually impossible for anyone who didn't already have money to make any. It was the Great Depression—a time when the stock market was uncertain and unstable, and many people struggled to find jobs to feed their families. For Black Americans, making money was particularly challenging. Segregation limited access to education and job opportunities. Banks were owned by white people—and Black folks were constantly denied loans even if they had the means to pay them back.[237] In his book *Playing the Numbers: Gambling in Harlem Between the Wars,* historian Stephen Roberts writes: "The reason [gambling] was the biggest Black business of the early 1900s is because Black Americans found it so hard to get involved in other legal businesses."[238]

But there was one way to make a quick buck. It was called the "numbers game."

Numbers, which was also called "policy" in some cities, was an illegal lottery that ran for decades in urban areas like New York, Chicago, and Boston. The idea behind the game was simple: you place a bet on a number between 1 and 999. The next day, a random number is generated at 10:00 a.m.—usually through a complicated process that was based on the transactions between banks at the New York Clearing House.[239] If you happened to bet on the right number, you would get payout based on your bet. If you didn't, you'd lose your money and try again the next day.

Anyone could start their own numbers game—all you needed was some cash to pay out winning numbers and a team of runners, who would travel through the neighborhood every afternoon collecting bets for the day. There were hundreds of games across the country, from small-time operations to big-name mobsters who would collect thousands of dollars a day in bets. The people who ran the numbers games would collect a betting fee—usually around 20 percent—which they kept as profit on any winnings.

For Stephanie St. Clair, who started running numbers in the mid-1920s, those betting fees were the beginning of a whole new life.

THE NUMBERS QUEEN

Not much is known about Stephanie St. Clair's early life—in part because she preferred to tell wild stories about herself in the dozens of newspaper ads she placed throughout the 1920s. She may have been an immigrant from the French-speaking island of Guadeloupe, but she told people that she was of "French European heritage" and came from France. She was born in the 1880s or 1890s, and traveled to Montreal, Quebec, in 1911, when she was a young woman. There is no record of her time in Quebec, but her biographer suspects she worked as a maid or a cook when she arrived. In 1912, she took a boat to New York and never looked back.

For the next ten years, St. Clair eked out a living in New York City. Not much is known about what she did during this time. But we do know that in the mid-1920s, something changed. Biographers suggest she might have won a lawsuit and received a large payout—or she might even have placed a winning numbers bet. But either way, St. Clair finally had some money to her name, and she used it to start her own gambling racket.[240]

St. Clair's business grew fast. In just a few months, she was making thousands of dollars a month. Many people believe that at the height of her success, she made $200,000 a year.[241] She employed as many as fifty runners to walk through Harlem taking bets each day, along with a team of clerks and messengers. By 1930, one journalist estimated that St. Clair had a fortune worth around $500,000, which would be nearly $8 million in today's money.[242]

With her wealth, St. Clair funded a lavish lifestyle—and many business ventures that would solidify her fortune for decades to come. She bought small apartment buildings in New York as a business investment, and she spent the rest of her money on beautiful coats, dresses, jewelry, and hats. She had a timeless elegance that made her a fashion icon, and though she made her money illegally, she wasn't interested in hiding from the world. St. Clair used to take out newspaper ads to share stories about her life, talk with her community, and even challenge enemy mobsters. In one of those ads she wrote: "I have received letters and telephone messages from men which have annoyed me very much ... I, Mme. St. Clair, am not looking for a husband or a sweetheart. If they do not stop annoying me, I shall publish their names and letters in the newspaper."[243]

St. Clair soon became a figure in Harlem. She was the Numbers Queen—but unfortunately, her reign was short-lived. In 1929, St. Clair was arrested for running numbers and spent a year in prison.[244] She handed her business over to her partner, a Black mobster named Ellsworth "Bumpy" Johnson. Her career was over. But even without numbers, St. Clair soon found a way to stay in the limelight.

"I AM SANE AND SMART AND FEARLESS"

Throughout the 1920s, St. Clair was a community leader in Harlem. She formed a group called the French Legal Society, which helped Black immigrants who had recently come to New York City. She placed ads in the newspapers that taught Black people about their legal rights, including their right to refuse a property search without a warrant. She also hired dozens of her neighbors, not only to serve as runners, but also as cooks, chauffeurs, property managers, and more. She took the money she made from the numbers game and gave it back to her community.[245]

After her arrest, St. Clair threw herself into her activism with a vengeance. She was known for her fiery temper, and she channeled her anger into her fight against police corruption in Harlem. As soon as she got out of prison, St. Clair began testifying that police in New York were harassing Black runners and benefitting from the illegal lottery. Because of her testimony, fourteen police officers were suspended.[246]

Next, St. Clair turned to the white mobsters who were trying to take over the numbers game in Harlem. In particular, she had her eye on a violent crime boss named Dutch Schultz. Schultz was a white mobster who was known for his brutality. He wasn't the kind of person you'd want to cross.

Like many white mobsters at the time, Schultz saw that Black people were making money off the numbers game in Harlem, and he wanted in on it. He started sending his men to the neighborhood to threaten Black and Hispanic runners to join his team and sell for him—if they didn't, he said, he would kill them. Schultz also had ins with the local police force. He paid police officers to arrest runners who didn't join him and to turn a blind eye to his attacks on the people of Harlem.

St. Clair saw what Schultz was doing, and she wasn't having any of it. Schultz may have been "Public Enemy Number One," but he was no match for St. Clair's rage. In an article in the *New York Post*, St. Clair declared war: "[I'm] not afraid of Dutch Schultz or any other living man. He'll never touch me! The policy game is my game. He took it away from me and is swindling the colored people. I'm the only one that's after him."[247]

For five years, St. Clair did battle with Dutch Schultz, whom she called "the Dutchman." She gathered a band of Black folks in Harlem who ran numbers games and started harassing white store owners who collected bets for Schultz. St. Clair herself smashed in store windows of owners who wouldn't stop running bets for her enemy. She and the other numbers runners would destroy bets, take bats to display cases, and cause as much chaos as they could muster. They were trying to run these store owners out of Harlem—and often, they succeeded.[248]

In 1935, St. Clair finally won her battle with Schultz. The mobster was shot in a bathroom in New Jersey—supposedly because he got on the bad side of an important member of the Mafia. On his deathbed, St. Clair sent her adversary a note. It read: "As ye sow, so shall you reap."[249]

The note was signed simply, "Madame Queen."

THE LAST DAYS OF MADAME QUEEN

After Dutch Schultz's death, St. Clair's life becomes a bit of a blur. In 1936, she got married—though not legally—to a man named Bishop Amiru Al-Mu-Minin Sufi Abdul Hamid. Hamid was a labor activist who fought for local business owners to hire Black workers in New York City. Like his new wife, he was a little eccentric. He claimed to be born "in the shadows of the Egyptian pyramids"[250] but was actually born in Massachusetts. He was one of the first Black activists to convert to Islam, and he was also known for being anti-Semitic. Most days, he wore turbans, velvet shirts, tall black boots, and a cape.

From the beginning, Hamid and St. Clair's marriage didn't go well. In 1937, St. Clair found out that Hamid was in love with a woman from Jamaica. She was livid. In a rage, she shot at him three times but didn't hit him. He pressed charges, and she was sentenced to two to ten years in prison for attempted murder. Despite the fact that St. Clair nearly killed a man, the judge expressed his admiration for her at the trial. "This woman," he said, "[has] been living by her wits all of her life."[251]

After she got out of prison, St. Clair fell out of the spotlight. No one knows much about her later years. One reporter for the *New York Post* interviewed her in 1960 and said she was living a "lavish lifestyle" in a four-story apartment in Harlem.[252] Other records show that she visited family in the Caribbean after leaving prison, and then she lived a life of seclusion before dying in a psychiatric hospital in 1969.[253]

But no matter how St. Clair spent her last few decades, her legacy remains. Stephanie St. Clair was a successful Black businesswoman at a time in history when it was almost impossible for Black people of any gender to break into the market. She was an immigrant who made a name for herself in New York society against all odds. She was an advocate for her community and her culture. She was passionate and fiery and not afraid to put up a fight for what she believed in. She was a gangster, and a free spirit, and a force to be reckoned with. And for almost a decade, she was the Queen of Numbers—a game that, one could argue, she won in the end.

CHAPTER THIRTEEN

HACKERS: HOW A FIFTEEN-YEAR-OLD SHUT DOWN NASA

On September 20, 2000, a sixteen-year-old boy sat behind the defendant's table in a federal courtroom in Miami, Florida. He was tall and skinny, with pale skin, dark hair, and round glasses. He looked just like any other teenager.

But Jonathan James wasn't just any kid. A year earlier, when he was only fifteen, he illegally accessed thousands of confidential emails from the US Department of Defense and shut down computers at NASA. And he did it all from the comfort of his desk chair.[254]

In 2000, Jonathan James became the first juvenile offender to be sentenced to prison time for committing a cybercrime. But he certainly wouldn't be the last young person to find himself in trouble with the law after a few hours in front of a computer screen. For as long as computers have existed, people have been finding ways to hack them—and the intentions of these hackers are often just as hard to trace as the evidence of their crimes.

HACKING NASA

According to stories on internet forums, which may or may not be true, Jonathan James's life as a hacker began innocently enough: he was trying to get around parental controls.

Jonathan's father was a computer systems analyst for nearly two decades, and Jonathan knew his way around a computer—a skill set that wasn't nearly as common back in the 1980s, when he was a kid. According to fans on the internet, Jonathan started getting interested in his dad's computer when he was around six years old. He liked to play computer games—so much so that his dad had to install parental controls to stop Jonathan from playing all night long. Those parental controls were supposedly Jonathan's first hacking test, and he passed with flying colors.[255]

As he got older, Jonathan kept fiddling with his dad's computer. He started teaching himself how operating systems work. From there, it was only a short leap to learn computer programming. Jonathan started by learning C, a coding language that was first developed in 1972 and is still used by programmers today.

In an interview with PBS, Jonathan explains that he taught himself everything he needed to know about computers: "Oh, [I learned coding] by reading, by talking to people. And by spending so much time on the computer, learning how it works, learning the source code and the programs and the commands ... I know Unix and C like the back of my hand, because I studied all these books, and I was on the computer for so long," he said.[256]

All that practice eventually led Jonathan to a new challenge: hacking into government computers. Government officials reported in court that between June and October 1999, Jonathan found his way through the back door of some very important networks—like the ones that control the International Space Station and the Defense Threat Reduction Agency, a branch of the US government that monitors threats to national security.[257]

First, on June 29 and 30, Jonathan hacked into the computers at NASA's Marshall Space Flight Center in Huntsville, Alabama. While in the NASA network, he stole data and downloaded software, which ultimately shut down thirteen computers for nearly three weeks.[258] Government officials also claim that some of the software Jonathan downloaded granted him access to technology on board the International Space Station. In his interview with PBS, Jonathan clarifies:

> No, [I couldn't have done anything with the international space station software]. It was for the environmental control program. Who wants that—you can play with the air conditioner, or what?" . . . The code itself was crappy. . . The only reason I was downloading the source code in the first place was because I was studying C programming. And what better way to learn than reading software written by the government?[259]

Later that year, between August and October, Jonathan hacked into government networks again—this time at the Defense Threat Reduction Agency. Supposedly, he intercepted more than three thousand confidential messages and had access to at least nineteen usernames and passwords of high-level government officials.

In an interview with a reporter, Jonathan's father, Robert, said: "'I've been in computers for 20 years, and I can't do what he was doing." Later in the interview, he defended his son. "He didn't do anything destructive," Robert said.[260]

Occasionally, Jonathan would get kicked off a government computer during one of his hacking sprees. The government clearly knew he was inside their networks—he just assumed they didn't care. Jonathan even claims that he got in touch with government network administrators to tell them that their systems were compromised. "I would email the system administrators sometimes and tell them that their computers were vulnerable. I would tell them how to break in, and how to fix the problems. I'd give them advice, and they would never follow it. Three weeks later I would go in and I still had access to their computers," he said.[261]

As it turns out, agents did care about Jonathan's emails. And they were using them to track him down. Ultimately, they used his IP address to trace him to his family's home in Miami.

"I never knew that they would actually come to my house," Jonathan told PBS. "Then ... my mom woke me from bed and said that the FBI was at the door ... I walk out and I see everybody with vests that say Federal Agents and NASA and DOD on the back with guns and all that good stuff."[262]

Agents questioned Jonathan for a few hours and took his computers away for investigation. He claims he apologized for what he did. "They told me not to do it again," Jonathan told PBS, "and if I do it again, I'll leave in handcuffs. But for now, they don't consider me a criminal."[263]

Then, three months later, they had another meeting. The FBI was thinking about pressing charges. They wanted to send a message to other hackers—to prove this kind of offense wouldn't go unnoticed.

In July 2000, Jonathan got a call from his father. The government was putting Jonathan on trial. That fall, Jonathan was sentenced to six months in prison, making him the first juvenile offender to be put away for cybercrime.

WHAT COLOR HAT WOULD YOU WEAR?

Just like cowboys in an old Western movie, you can tell a lot about a hacker based on the color of their (metaphorical) hat.

Within the industry, hackers are separated into three groups: white hats, black hats, and gray hats. White-hat hackers are the good guys. Companies pay white-hat hackers to dive into their networks and find weak spots—then, the hackers report back on what they found, so network owners can build up their defenses and keep other, more malicious intruders out.[264]

Black-hat hackers, on the other hand, are the villains of cybercrime. They hack into networks with malicious intent—usually they want money, power, or confidential information. Black-hat hackers might release malware that destroys files or shuts down entire networks for weeks. They might also steal your personal information, like your credit card number or your passwords. Black-hat hackers may work alone or join a criminal organization, but no matter who they work for, their end goal is to wreak havoc and get paid.[265] And unfortunately, because they rarely leave any evidence of their crimes behind, black-hat hackers are almost impossible to stop.

Like most crimes, however, hacking isn't always black or white. Hackers like Jonathan James are called "gray hats," because their behavior falls somewhere between hero and villain—they aren't always following the rules, but they aren't trying to hurt anyone either. And that complexity can make it hard for law enforcement to know what to do with them. In an anonymous interview with PBS that took place just before he was sent to prison, Jonathan James said:

> Six months ... it's not as long as some other sentences, [but] it's still a long time. And that's six months of me being surrounded by people that did these actual crimes, did bad things to other people, to humanity. I think the appropriate response [to my behavior] would be perhaps to take my computers away like [the government] did, and leave it at that. They could tell me that I can't use the internet for a while, to teach me a lesson, teach me that they actually do care about what I'm doing, and that I shouldn't do it again. But they shouldn't put the youth of America in jail.[266]

BECOMING ANONYMOUS

Jonathan James died in 2008 in his home in Pinecrest, Florida, when he was only twenty-four years old.[267] But in the eight years between his trial and his death, he got to witness the rise of a new group of young hackers eager to show off their skills. That group, which is still operational today, is called Anonymous.

Anonymous is an informal group—there's no official way to become a member. Basically, if you say you're a part of Anonymous, then you are. The group started on a forum called "4chan" in 2003, and their name comes from the default username given to anyone who posts on 4chan without an account. Anonymous has no manifesto, and there is no formal leader. The only thing banding these hackers together is their commitment to a practice they call "hacktivism."[268]

The hacktivists, or hacker-activists, who make up Anonymous use their technical skills to fight for political causes. They typically target right-wing or conservative organizations. Anonymous made the news for the first time in 2008 when a group of hacktivists protested the Church of Scientology. The group banded together to create a denial-of-service attack—which is essentially a cyberattack in which hackers visit a site repeatedly until the servers crash and the site is temporarily shut down. They also posted videos on YouTube about their mission and protested outside churches wearing their signature Guy Fawkes masks,[269] which are based on a portrait of a famous Spanish rebel who was arrested in 1605 after trying to blow up the British Parliament. Anonymous adopted the mask because it symbolizes standing up against authority.[270]

Since 2008, the group has been involved in dozens of causes. They appeared at Occupy Wall Street protests, hacked into the US Senate, and famously posted a video threatening the Minneapolis Police Department after the death of George Floyd in 2020. In the video, one hacker in a Guy Fawkes mask with a distorted voice says: "Greetings, citizens of the United States. This is a message from Anonymous to the Minneapolis Police Department. We will be exposing your many crimes to the world. We are legion. Expect us."[271]

Members of Anonymous often break the law—and many have been thrown in prison for their crimes.[272] But for many of these hacktivists, their crimes aren't about causing chaos or destruction. They are about making the world a better place. One member of Anonymous, a hacker named Chris Doyon, revealed his identity to the world in 2011. He compared his work with Anonymous to the Civil Rights Movement, saying that hacktivism is "no different, really, than taking up seats at the Woolworth lunch counters."[273]

Later that year, Doyon told reporters: "I am immensely proud, and humbled to the core, to be a part of the idea called Anonymous. All you need to be a world-class hacker is a computer and a cool pair of sunglasses. And the computer is optional."[274]

CYBER VILLAINS, CYBER HEROES

In an interview with PBS, Jonathan James said:

> [Hacking] is power at your fingertips. You can control all these computers from the government, from the military, from large corporations. And if you know what you're doing, you can travel through the internet at your will, with no restrictions ... It's intellectual. It stimulates my mind. It's a challenge.[275]

Hackers have many reasons for doing what they do—some are villains, some are heroes, and most fall somewhere in between. But no matter what their motives are, hackers have the power to change our world. They can fight dictators and expose criminals. They can shut down oil pipelines or infiltrate the international space station.

What they choose to do with their skills, at the end of the day, is entirely up to them.

CHAPTER FOURTEEN

THE REIGN OF THE PIRATE QUEEN

In 1810, a woman stepped off a ship on the shores of Canton, China. With her was a small entourage of women and children who had traveled with her by boat. She walked with purpose toward the governor general's headquarters. She had a meeting to attend.[276]

The governor's home had been turned into a fortress in preparation. Soldiers surrounded the building, their teeth clenched. They had their weapons drawn. They were ready for a fight. For this woman, who walked unarmed through the streets of Canton, was not just any sailor. She was the most fearsome pirate history has ever known.

Though the real name of the pirate queen Ching Shih has been lost to history, her story has not. In her heyday, she had one hundred times more ships than the notorious pirate Blackbeard—and nearly two hundred times as many pirates under her command.[277]

But to truly understand Ching Shih's legacy, we must go all the way back to 1650—when the Golden Age of Piracy began.

PIRATES!

Pirates have been roaming the seven seas for more than two thousand years, since the time of the ancient Greeks. But most pirate stories are associated with a period between 1650 and 1730, when there were said to be more than five thousand buccaneers watching for merchant ships heavy with treasure and precious cargo. Some of the most famous of these pirates included Henry Morgan, William "Captain" Kidd, and Edward Teach, also known as Blackbeard, who commanded four ships and three hundred to four hundred pirates in his two-year career as the most fearsome pirate in America.[278]

Historians believe that the Golden Age of Piracy was the result of an increase in trade across the Atlantic Ocean. During this time, European countries were transporting goods to and from their colonies in Africa, the Caribbean, North America, and beyond. Many of the boats were full of treasures—not just money, but also expensive products like sugar and tea. Pirates noticed those boats and saw an opportunity. If they could take down the boat, the treasures were ripe for the plucking.

Pirates were particularly active in the Caribbean. When Spanish colonizers took over parts of the Americas, including Florida, Mexico, and the Caribbean islands, they found that the ground was full of gold, silver, and gemstones.[279] That precious cargo was shipped on Spanish galleons (large multi-deck sailboats) back to Europe for the king to enjoy. But once pirates got a taste of those jewels, they couldn't get enough. Soon, pirate attacks were so common on Spanish galleons that they had to travel in fleets, with armed boats at the ready to ward off the greedy pirates.

But who were these pirates? And why would anyone want to become one? The reality is that for many people in Europe, piracy was simply their best option for survival. Farmers were being pushed off their land by rich landowners, and small business owners in cities were being put out of business by their larger competitors. It was hard to get a job. Even if you wanted to learn a trade, like blacksmithing or leatherwork, you would have to work for seven years as an apprentice before you would make any money. People were desperate—so they turned to the sea.[280]

Many pirates were poor sailors who wanted to take charge of their own lives—and get rich quick. Some pirates began their careers as privateers—private sailors who are paid by the military to join their fleet and fight for a particular country during a war. Once the war ended, it wasn't hard to keep attacking other boats—except this time, you'd keep all the treasures for yourself.[281]

The Golden Age of Piracy ended in 1730, just a few years after the famous pirate Blackbeard was killed by the US Navy off the coast of North Carolina. But piracy was certainly not over—not even close. In fact, the career of the most successful pirate in history wouldn't even begin for another eighty years, when Ching Shih took over the South China Sea.[282]

THE WIDOW OF CHENG I

Historians know almost nothing about Ching Shih, whose pirate fleet was more powerful than the Chinese navy. We don't know when or where she was born, though most experts believe she was probably from the city of Canton in South China. We don't even know her real name—she is simply known as Ching Shih or Zheng Yi Sao, which means "the widow of Cheng I."[283]

What we do know about Ching Shih's life starts in 1801, when she marries the notorious pirate captain Zheng Yi. She met Cheng I when she was working on a flower boat, a floating brothel popular with sailors in Canton. Ching Shih was one of the entertainers on the boat. When Cheng I saw her, he immediately fell in love. But Ching Shih was a smart businesswoman—she knew that Cheng I could offer her a leg up in a world with few opportunities for women. When he asked for her hand in marriage, she had one condition: She wanted half of his fortune. Cheng I agreed, and the two were wed.[284]

Ching Shih and Cheng I began their marriage by joining the Tay Son rebellion in Vietnam as privateers. During the Tay Son rebellion, working-class people revolted against the government. The

Vietnamese revolutionaries paid Chinese pirates to fight alongside them. But the rebellion was more than just a quick job for Cheng I and his crew. It also trained the pirates to fight—and gave Cheng I an idea. He realized that if they joined together, these trained Chinese pirates would be a force to be reckoned with. So he and Ching Shih set out to create a united pirate fleet. By 1805, they had seven separate fleets, each named after the color of their flag. Each fleet had its own captain, and every captain reported to Cheng I.[285]

For two years, Cheng I was the leader of the pirate fleet. But around 1807, he died. Experts aren't sure whether he died in a storm or while fighting at sea, but suddenly Cheng I's massive gang of pirates had no leader.

There were few female pirates in Europe and America because for centuries, men thought it was bad luck for women to work on ships. But in China, many women lived their lives on the sea. Working-class women often captained boats called "sampans," which were floating shops that traveled up and down the coast of China. It was also common for wives to work at sea alongside their husbands. If the captain of a boat died at sea, his wife would often take over—which is why few pirates complained when Ching Shih took the wheel and began her reign as the pirate queen.[286]

CHING SHIH'S CODE

When Ching Shih took control of the fleet, she didn't just follow in her husband's footsteps. She did things her own way. First, she put the pirate Cheung Po Tsai in charge of the red fleet, which was by far the most powerful branch of her pirate empire. Cheung Po Tsai would eventually become her husband. Then, Ching Shih set about growing her pirate army. When Cheng I was in charge, he commanded about fifty thousand pirates. Ching Shih added another twenty thousand pirates, making her fleet the largest in history—and bigger than nearly all official navies at the time.[287]

Ching Shih had a strict code of conduct for her crew. If a pirate went to shore twice without her permission, he would be put to death. He would also be put to death for disobeying a superior officer. Ching Shih also had strict rules around romantic relationships on board. Men could marry women they met on shore, but they had to be loyal to those women. Ching Shih knew that romantic relationships could cause chaos and tension on board. If a pirate was not loyal to his wife, he would be killed—and so would his new girlfriend.[288]

To make money, Ching Shih had a relatively simple system. She knew that sailors were worried about being attacked by pirates, so she offered them protection—for a price. Captains would pay Ching Shih in exchange for a guarantee of safety. Her fleet would not attack them, and if another boat launched an attack, Ching Shih would pay the captain a settlement to cover their losses. It was essentially a pirate insurance policy. At the height of her power, even small villages on the coast paid Ching Shih to avoid pirate attacks.

The Chinese government knew that Ching Shih ruled the South China Sea, but they weren't powerful enough to do anything about it. For years, China tried to fight Ching Shih and take over her pirate fleet. But Ching Shih won every battle. Finally, out of desperation, the Chinese government even changed their strict foreign policy, which had prohibited doing business with Europe, to ask the English and Portuguese for help. Portugal sent over six battleships, called men-of-war, to help the Chinese fight off Ching Shih. Ching Shih and her gang sunk them all.[289]

THE FIGHT FOR THE RED FLEET

After years of evading capture and ruling over the coasts of China, trouble struck the pirate fleet. But it didn't come from the government. It came from inside Ching Shih's own ranks.

The conflict began when the captain of the black fleet decided he wanted the more powerful red fleet for himself. Tensions stewed as Ching Shih tried to put the unruly captain in his place—but he wouldn't back down. He decided that there was an easy way to get what he wanted. He would go to the Chinese government.[290]

After so many failed attempts to take down Ching Shih, the government knew that only another pirate could fight her. They promised that any buccaneer who could help end the pirate queen's reign would be granted their freedom, no matter how heinous their crimes. The captain of the black fleet began working with the Chinese government to capture Ching Shih—but unfortunately for him, Ching Shih was as smart as she was courageous. She decided the best way to solve this problem was to give the government what they wanted. So she made an appointment with the governor general himself.[291]

On that fateful day in 1810, Ching Shih disembarked from her ship without weapons. She walked confidently toward the governor general's headquarters, smiling and nodding at the anxious soldiers pointing their swords in her direction. She knew she held all the power. And the Chinese government knew it, too.

In her discussion with the governor general, Ching Shih made a shocking deal. She promised to stand down—but only for the right price. She wanted the pirates to keep their fortunes, and she wanted the Chinese government to pay every single one of her seventy thousand crew members a salary to help them return to society. She asked that pirates be allowed to join the military if they wanted—they already had fighting skills, after all—and demanded that no pirate be imprisoned for their crimes.

The government, desperate to take control of the coast, agreed.

In her chapter on Ching Shih, author and historian Laura Sook Duncombe writes, "[Ching Shih's] pirates would die warm in their beds, covered in cozy quilts bought on the government dime."[292]

PIRATE WOMEN: A LEGACY

Ching Shih died in 1844 when she was sixty-nine years old. Though we don't know much about her final decades, experts do know that she lived a life of comfort with her husband Cheung Po Tsai thanks to her business prowess and negotiation skills. Even in her quiet retirement, she maintained her legacy as the most successful and fearsome pirate of all time.

Though Ching Shih had the largest pirate empire, she certainly wasn't the only female pirate to rule the Seven Seas. Anne Bonny was an Irish woman who moved to the Bahamas with her pirate husband in the early 1700s. She was known for wild red hair and her hot temper. When her ship was captured by English forces, her last words to her husband, Calico Jack Rackham, were: "Sorry to see you there, but if you'd fought like a man, you would not have been hang'd like a dog."

Sailing alongside Anne Bonny was Mary Read, a female pirate who dressed like a man to avoid detection aboard ship. Supposedly, only Anne and Calico Jack knew Mary Read's true identity. Mary and Anne were close friends, and may have even had a romantic relationship.[293]

In Morocco, the female pirate Sayyida al Hurra ruled the western coast in the mid-1500s as the ally of the fearsome pirate Barbarossa. [294] In the Caribbean, Anne Dieu-le-Veut became a pirate when she married a Dutch buccaneer named Laurens de Graaf, who fell in love with her after she challenged him to a duel.[295] We don't often hear about female pirates, but they made their mark on maritime history. In fact, pirate women can be found in nearly every corner of world history, if you take the time to look.

CHAPTER FIFTEEN

WHAT WE CAN LEARN FROM BONES

Sometimes people die, and nobody knows what happened.

They might be the victims of a crime, or they might have had an unexpected medical emergency. They might have died a long time ago—sometimes hundreds of years in the past—and only their bones are left behind. But regardless of what happened to them, someone must solve the mystery of their death. For people living in Washington State, that person is twenty-six-year-old Kristen Smith.

Kristen Smith is a medicolegal death investigator for Pierce County in Washington. She calls herself a "Last Responder," because she spends her days trying to piece together what happens after someone dies. "I am not driving up in an ambulance to save someone's life in the knick of time," Kristen says. "But I am showing up in the aftermath to try to find closure for families. It's my job to do a thorough investigation, and hopefully find justice for someone."

Kristen's work might take her to the top of Mount Rainier, or just down the road to the local hospital. But no matter where she's working that day, Kristen is committed to one thing: advocating for victims who can no longer speak for themselves. "I get to be a voice for someone who doesn't have their voice anymore," she says.

In this chapter, we'll follow Kristen into the field as she reveals what it's like to work as a forensic death investigator—and what she has learned from spending many hours a day in the company of bones.

A DAY IN THE LIFE OF A DEATH INVESTIGATOR

According to the medical examiner's office, there are five manners of death: natural, accident, homicide, suicide, and undetermined. It is Kristen's job to find out which of these applies in each case. Sometimes, the answer is obvious—but sometimes, it's much harder to uncover. If the medical examiner or the police suspect that a death might not be natural, Kristen gets a phone call. From that point on, it's her job to speak for the victim.

Kristen's investigations often start in her car as she travels to the scene of the incident. On the way, she calls law enforcement, who decide whether they want to put a detective on the case. Many people are surprised to learn that when a person dies, police don't have the right to move or touch the body. They have to wait for an investigator like Kristen to arrive.

At the scene, Kristen works either by herself or with law enforcement officers to gather evidence and make note of any clues that might help her determine the cause of death. She might look at the pill bottles on the person's nightstand to learn about any health conditions they had, or study the location and placement of objects in the room. Often, she interviews their family members to learn about the victim—who they are, what they were doing that day, and what circumstances might have led to their death.

Once she's collected all the evidence she can, Kristen returns to her office. She reads medical records, downloads the photos she took on the scene, and compiles all her evidence. Then, she asks herself: What happened here? What is the story this person would want me to tell?

Sometimes, if law enforcement or a family member can't identify a victim, it's also Kristen's job to find out who they are. If she's lucky, a victim will have a driver's license or other identifying information on them—but the medical examiner's office likes to confirm the identity of every victim before they sign a death certificate. It is Kristen's job to find out the identities of these people, who would otherwise have no names.

To find the identities of these unnamed victims, Kristen often relies on her training in forensic anthropology. She knows that you can learn a lot about a person by studying their bones—and on days when she is identifying a victim, she puts those skills to the test.

Usually, Kristen starts by taking fingerprints, which she sends to the FBI to run through a database. If she's lucky, she will find a match in the system—but that doesn't always happen. If fingerprints fail, Kristen will look for a driver's license or credit card. She can use a person's name to search for their medical history. Then, she can use those records to find out important identifying information about them—like their dental records or whether they have ever broken any bones. She uses X-rays to study their bones and determine if her victim matches the person in the file.

If a person doesn't have a fingerprint match and Kristen can't find any identifying documents that reveal their name, she has to rely on their body to tell their story. Dental records, chest X-rays, and other tools can help differentiate one victim from another—sometimes people might be identified based on a tattoo on their arm, or the filling in their tooth, or the wrist they broke in the second grade. Each person is unique, and their body tells a story. As a death investigator, Kristen knows how to bring those stories to life.

FOR THE LOVE OF BONES

How does a person become a forensic death investigator? For Kristen, her love of bones began when she was in middle school—but she wasn't obsessed with skeletons. At least, not at first. Back then, she read every book on Egyptian mummies she could get her hands on. She was fascinated, in particular, by how the ancient Egyptians treated their dead. From there, her interest grew: from mummies to the skeletal system and finally to forensics.

"I was always interested in medicine," Kristen says, "but I was squeamish. The idea of working on living people freaked me out." But she didn't feel squeamish about death. "Forensic anthropology allowed me to learn a lot of the same knowledge about anatomy and the human body that doctors and nurses learn, but I could apply it in a totally different way," she explains.

After high school, Kristen went to college at New Mexico State to study biological anthropology. In school, she learned not just about anatomy, but also about history and culture. She studied how people lived by examining their skeletons and the artifacts they were buried alongside. She learned about different kinds of burial practices and the spiritual beliefs behind them. During college, Kristen even got to study abroad at a field school in Romania, where she helped experts excavate the bones of Romanians who died in the 1700s.

Then, after college, Kristen hit a slump. She struggled to find a job in anthropology. "In the US, most of our 'ancient populations' are Native American," Kristen explains, "and there are laws in place to protect Native American remains and ensure they are safely returned to their tribes. That means that most forensic anthropologists have to work in places like Europe, where there are more jobs because people have been living there for centuries."

Kristen didn't want to move to Europe, but she did want to put her degree to good use. She started thinking about one of her old passions: forensics. She had minored in forensics in college, and she thought she could find a job that excited her in that field. Soon, she was back in school—this time at the University of Florida, where she got a master's degree in forensic science with a focus in forensic medicine.

But even with a master's degree, it still wasn't easy for Kristen to get a job. "The field of forensics is very competitive," she says. "There's plenty of work to do—but the government hasn't created enough jobs. We are twenty or thirty years behind where we should be, and that makes it tough for people to find a job, especially if they are new to the field."

For two straight years, Kristen applied for jobs in forensics. She went to dozens of interviews, but even the ones that seemed promising didn't end in a job offer. In the meantime, she spent her time helping the living. She worked for a mental health nonprofit in Vermont, where she is from, and as a victim's advocate for people who have experienced domestic violence. But as much as she loved those jobs, she knew they weren't her calling. So she kept applying, and applying, and applying.

And then, finally, there was a light at the end of the tunnel. Kristen applied for a temporary job in North Carolina. "It was going to be my last chance," she says. "I had applied to so many jobs, and I was just tired. I didn't think it was going to happen for me." But this time, it did happen. Kristen got the job. She moved down to North Carolina and started working as a forensic death investigator. And then, after a few months, another job opened up. This one was in Tacoma, Washington. She applied. She got the job.

Just like that, Kristen packed up her Jeep and headed west. After years of waiting, she was finally living her dream—and she hasn't looked back since.

"THERE'S NO TIMELINE ON FOLLOWING YOUR DREAMS"

Kristen knows her job isn't for everybody. It is often exhausting—in fact, she had to reschedule our first interview because she worked for sixteen hours straight after an unexpected emergency call, and then went back into work only eight hours later. But for Kristen, the long hours are worth it because she's making a difference. She doesn't just study bones. She helps tell people's last stories. For her, that mission is worth two years of job applications and dashed hopes.

"It is hard to get into this field," she says. "But if you're passionate about anything, you keep finding ways to do what you want to do.

"I want kids to know that even if something is hard, it will pay off in the end. For two years, I told people I would never get a job in forensics. And every time they told me it would happen someday, I would get angry, because I thought they didn't get it. They didn't see how hard it was, and how hopeless. But now, I'm on the other side, doing what I always imagined I'd do. Those people who encouraged me were right all along.

"There's no timeline on following your dreams," Kristen adds. "If it takes years, or even decades, that's okay. You just keep working at it. You keep learning and growing. Even if you think what you're doing will never get you where you want to go, you never know the full story. I am always shocked by what knowledge will come in handy when I'm out working a case."

TEN FAST FACTS ABOUT BONES

Want to learn more about bones? Here are ten facts from Kristen to get you started.

1. When babies are born, they have more than 300 bones. As they grow, some of those bones fuse together to form the 206 bones that make up an adult skeleton.

2. A skull can teach you a lot more than you might think. If you are holding a skull, you can uncover someone's age, biological sex, genetic history, and ethnicity.

3. Another way to determine someone's biological sex is by looking at their pelvis, because men and women have differently shaped pelvic bones. You can also tell if a woman had more than two children by the shape of her pelvis.

4. You can tell the difference between a human and an animal bone based on the weight, shape, size, and density of the bone.

5. Skeletons can't speak—but their teeth can tell you how they lived and what they ate. For example, we know that rich people in Europe in the 1700s ate more sugar than poor people, because their teeth are often rotten or missing.

6. You can tell whether someone had access to a doctor or not by studying how their bones have healed. For example, forensic anthropologists can tell if someone had a broken bone set using a cast or splint, or if it healed naturally.

7. Forensic anthropologists have to learn the name of every bone in the body—but that's not all. Every single bone also has unique features that forensic anthropologists must be able to identify. If you look at a bone, every groove, bump, and arch has a name.

8. The smallest bone in your body is called the stapes, and it's located inside your ear.

9. One of Kristen's favorite bones is the atlas vertebra, which holds up your skull. It's named after the story of Atlas, a titan in Greek mythology who held the weight of the world in his hands.

10. If you don't brush your teeth, a forensic anthropologist can tell! The plaque on your teeth can ossify, which means that it hardens over time and becomes a part of your skeleton.

PART TWO

THE DETECTIVE'S HANDBOOK

IDENTIFYING SUSPECTS WITH FINGERPRINT ANALYSIS

One of the most important observations that detectives make about a suspect isn't subjective at all: They take each character's fingerprints. Fingerprints are identifying marks, and they can tell us a lot about where characters have been and who was present at the scene of the crime. But how do they work?

In this activity, you will take your own fingerprints using an ink pad and learn how to compare them to fingerprints you pick up from a surface in your house or classroom. Then, you'll learn how to compare your two sets of prints using fingerprint pattern analysis.

Supplies:

- A glass cup
- Baby powder
- Makeup brushes
- Clear packing tape
- Dark construction paper (ideally black)
- Card stock
- An ink pad
- Magnifying glass

STEP 1: PICKING UP PRINTS

1. Assemble your supplies: a glass cup, baby powder, makeup brushes, clear packing tape, and construction paper.

2. Start by pressing your finger (ideally your thumb or pointer finger) onto the glass cup. Make sure you press firmly, so you leave a good print behind.

3. Carefully tap a small amount of baby powder onto the place where you left your print. You want just enough to cover the print with a fine coat of powder.

4. Using the makeup brush, carefully wipe away the extra powder to reveal the outline of your fingerprint on the glass.

5. Take a small piece of packing tape and press it over the fingerprint outline on your cup. Try to go smoothly from one side to the other, so you don't ruin the print.

6. Finally, attach your tape with the fingerprint outline to a piece of black construction paper to preserve it. You should be able to see the white outline of your print against the dark paper. If you can't see the fine lines in your fingerprint, you can always wipe off your glass and try again!

STEP 2: CAUGHT RED-HANDED

Now you've found a print at the scene of a crime. But if you don't have fingerprints to compare it with, you'll never identify a suspect. That means it's time to add some prints to our database.

1. Gather your supplies: card stock and ink pad.

2. Carefully roll your fingers over the ink pad, so the ink covers your whole fingertip.

3. Press each finger into your card stock, pushing firmly to make a clear imprint.

4. Complete this process for each finger to make a full set of fingerprints.

5. Label your prints in the bottom corner of the page with your full name and the date.

STEP 3: FINGERPRINT ANALYSIS

It's time to analyze those prints and compare the patterns to identify whether you have a match. While we have computer software that does this now, in the early days of fingerprint analysis, detectives did all this comparison by hand.

1. Before you begin, you need to know the basics of fingerprint analysis. There are three main shapes you can find in your fingerprints: loops, arches, and whorls. Check out the image below to compare the different shapes:

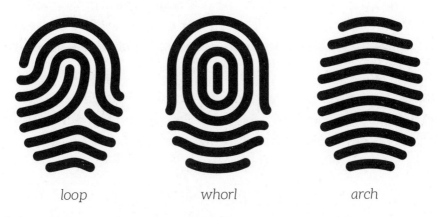

loop   *whorl*   *arch*

2. Once you feel confident about each pattern, it's time to take a look at your prints. Using the magnifying glass, look closely at the lines you see in the fingerprint you found on the glass. Then, compare them to the patterns in your set of fingerprints. Do they look similar? How can you tell?

3. If you have a friend or classmate with you, ask them to take their fingerprints, too. Then, compare how their fingerprint pattern differs from yours. Can you identify your culprit?

THE ART OF EAVESDROPPING

Detectives don't get all their information from the interrogation room. Sometimes, you come by critical clues in a slightly less obvious way—by being in the right place at the right time and observing the world around you. In this lab, we'll practice honing our observation skills with a timeless art: eavesdropping.

For this activity, you don't technically need any supplies, but I recommend a notebook, a pen or pencil, and some props that will help you look inconspicuous as you jot down clues (like a book or magazine to "read," some sunglasses to hide your face, or a false mustache).

1. Decide on your ideal eavesdropping location. It should be relatively crowded, so you can find subjects to observe and blend in without being noticed. Malls, cafeterias, coffee shops, and busy hallways can all be great places to eavesdrop.

2. Station yourself in an inconspicuous location (a place where you won't be easily noticed). Busy yourself with an activity, like checking your cell phone if you have one, reading a book, or just twiddling your thumbs. But don't actually focus your attention on your activity. Instead, open up your ears and see if you can hear any interesting snippets of conversation happening around you.

3. Now, it's time to practice observing. Choose one person or conversation to tune in to. What do you hear? You can also glance over to see who is talking and what they look like. What is their body language telling you? What information can you gather from context clues?

4. If you are reading a book, you might sneak your notebook inside the pages and take some casual notes about what you hear. You can also take notes on your cell phone if you want to be even sneakier.

5. Repeat this exercise three or four times, taking a few minutes to listen each time.

6. After you're done, compile your notes and see what you've found. Have you uncovered any mysteries? What about any ideas for stories? You can use your notes to imagine what might be happening in the lives of strangers.

7. BONUS: Take your notes and turn them into a short story or a play by creating characters and imagining what might have led them to have the conversation you overheard. If you do this, don't forget to change the names of your sources and keep their identifying information private. A detective's case file needs to stay secret to protect the investigation!

HOW TO WRITE YOUR OWN TRUE CRIME STORY

Have you ever heard of the term "armchair detective"? An armchair detective is a person who isn't actually at the scene of the crime—they just read about clues in the newspaper from the comfort of their own home and try to uncover a mystery using their wits.

I was an armchair detective while I wrote this book, and you can be an armchair detective, too, if you have an idea for a story and access to the internet. Here's how you can start writing your own true crime stories:

1. Find a story

Every good true crime book starts with a story. You might find story ideas from a documentary film, a podcast, or an article you read online. Maybe you hear about a crime in your neighborhood and decide you want to investigate. You can also find ideas for stories in a special place in your local newspaper called the "police blotter," where police departments report all the calls they responded to in the last week.

2. Make sure it's true

There are a lot of amazing mystery stories out there, but not all of them are true. True crime stories are nonfiction, which means that they are based on real events that happened in the world. If you hear about a story in a movie or from your neighbors, make sure it's true before you dive in to investigate.

3. Research, research, research

Most of writing a true crime story isn't writing at all. It's all about doing research. If you turn to the very back of this book, you'll find about three hundred endnotes, also called citations. That's a record of all the research I did to tell these fifteen stories. The best place to start with research is a reliable source, like a newspaper article or a book. Websites like Wikipedia can be a great place to start your research process and learn the basics of a case, but be careful: Information on Wikipedia isn't always accurate. Make sure you find other sources to back up anything you find on websites like Wikipedia. Many Wikipedia articles list their sources at the end of the web page. You can jump directly to those for more information.

If you can't find much information online, you might have to roll up your sleeves and do some investigating of your own! With your parents' permission, you can conduct interviews and make your own observations by visiting the scene of the crime. Remember that if a crime is recent, you may also need to contact local authorities to ensure you won't harm their investigation.

4. Consider all sides of the story

After you've done thorough research, it's time to review your notes. What are the many perspectives on this story? Are there any sources that contradict each other? Why might that be? It's important to consider all the sides of the story before you move forward. What do you think the victim might say about the story? What about the perpetrator—or the detective on the case? What side of the story do you want to tell?

5. Find your hook

Every great true crime story starts with a compelling introduction. Writers call this a "hook." What is the most interesting part of your story? Is there an action scene that you can start with? How about a character you can introduce? Are there any twists you can reveal to keep us guessing? The goal of a hook is to leave readers with questions that only you, the author, can answer.

6. Build tension

True crime stories are mysteries, and mysteries are fun to read because we need to know what happens. One of the ways authors keep you on the edge of your seat is by building tension. To build tension, don't reveal all the information you have in the first paragraph. Instead, set the scene. Introduce us to these characters. Ask questions. Add in some surprising twists and turns, if you can. Don't tell us how it all turns out until the very end.

7. Tell us why it matters

Finally, great true crime stories aren't just mysteries. They also make us think. Why do you think your story is important to tell? Did it make you think about the world differently? Did anything in it surprise you, or make you question your values or beliefs? How can you encourage your reader to think about this crime in a new way?

If you have a true crime story you'd like to share, send it my way. You can get in touch with me at morecuriouscases@gmail.com.

TRUE CRIME
TEACHER'S GUIDE

True crime is a complex genre. Many people dislike it because they associate it with TV shows that take advantage of victims and their families. Other people love the draw of a good mystery but don't think there's anything meaty to discuss. But people who really know and appreciate true crime understand that these stories tell us something about ourselves—what we value, what we are afraid of, how we treat others, and how we punish those who don't follow the rules.

Teaching kids about true crime is all about reminding them that these stories are never as simple as they seem on the surface. Kids are taught from an early age to see things as black-and-white, good or evil. But as we all know, there is no good or evil person. Everyone has complicated motivations behind their actions, which are influenced by their background, their circumstances, and their values.

I've included this short guide to provide some background on teaching true crime and encourage teachers to think about how they want to discuss these cases with their students. Though many of these cases are whimsical stories, others point to more serious questions, like: Who is a criminal? How should people (including children) be punished for their crimes? When does a harmless prank become malicious? And what should we do when someone does good work in their community through illegal means?

This teaching guide includes crime statistics you should know before talking to your students about the legal system. It also includes resources to learn more about teaching true crime, police abolition, prison reform, and other hot-button topics shaping true crime today.

Finally, I've included a list of discussion questions you can use to guide conversations with students, and links to external resources (including many podcasts I used to write these stories) that you can use in your classroom.

CRIME STATISTICS YOU SHOULD KNOW

1. Theft is the most common crime in the United States. Murder is the least common. Only about five in 100,000 people are victims of murder in the US.[296]

2. Both violent and nonviolent crime in the US has gone down significantly since the 1990s. Many sources show that crime rates have been cut in half in the last forty years.[297]

3. Even though crime has gone down for the last forty years, most people think it's going up. In twenty surveys conducted by Gallup from 1993 to 2019, at least 60 percent of US adults have said that crime has gone up nationally from the year before. That being said, most people don't think crime is going up where they live.[298]

4. Less than half of the crimes in the US are reported to police, and less than half of the crimes that do get reported are solved.[299]

5. You are much more likely to be the victim of a crime if you are younger or from a lower income bracket. Otherwise, your chances of being the victim of a crime are about equal no matter your race or gender.[300]

6. According to the National Alliance on Mental Illness, Black people are 2.1 times more likely to be arrested than white people, 3.5 times more likely to be incarcerated in a jail, and nearly five times more likely to go to prison. However, studies consistently show that the majority of crimes are committed by white people.[301]

7. At least one quarter of people who are currently incarcerated have been diagnosed with a severe mental illness. At least half of prisoners report having at least one mental health problem.[302]

ORGANIZATIONS WORKING ON CRIMINAL JUSTICE REFORM

- The Black Lives Matter movement
- The Marshall Project
- NAMI (National Alliance on Mental Illness)
- The Sentencing Project
- The Innocence Project

RESOURCES TO TEACH THESE STORIES

1. *Criminal* podcast with Phoebe Judge

- Episodes referenced in this book:
  - » "Masterpiece"
  - » "The Escape"
  - » "Ghost Racket Crusade"
  - » "The Clearwater Monster"
  - » "Spiritual Developments"
- Other episodes that are great for kids:
  - » "Kids on the Case"
  - » "Masquerade"
  - » "How to Sell a Haunted House"

2. *Ooh, You're in Trouble* podcast by Merk Nguyen

- A kid-friendly podcast about why people do things they aren't supposed to do, and what happens afterward.

3. *Escape from Alcatraz* (movie)

- A classic Clint Eastwood film to accompany the "Escaping Alcatraz" chapter. Good for ages 14+ according to Common Sense Media because of some profanity and violence.

4. *Last Seen* podcast from WBUR

- A series about the Gardner Museum heist. The podcast is not designed for kids, so share with caution, but many episodes are kid friendly and give detailed background on this case, and the people involved in it.

5. "The Feather Thief" from *This American Life*

- An hour-long podcast on the Tring feather heist, including interviews with Long Nguyen and other key players in the story.

6. "How Good Are You at Detecting Bias?" from KQED

- A full lesson plan with an interactive quiz to help students learn about different kinds of cognitive bias—a critical part of detective work.

7. *The Cottingley Fairy Photographs*

- These photos are available in the public domain, so kids can see what the photographs that Elsie and Frances took actually looked like.

8. Mumler's spirit photography

- Examples of Mumler's photos are widely available online and can be found on the Getty Museum website.

DISCUSSION QUESTIONS

CHAPTER ONE: THE DISAPPEARANCE OF MASTERPIECE THE POODLE

1. What is most valuable to you in the world? Would it be valuable to other people? Why or why not?

2. Do you think Masterpiece had a good life? Why or why not?

3. What do you think happened to Masterpiece? What evidence do you have to support your theory?

CHAPTER TWO: A THIEF IN THE DUTCH ROOM

1. If you were a detective on this case, what would you do about the fact that so many of the witnesses aren't reliable? Who would you believe, and why?

2. Why is it important that we preserve art?

3. Why do you think the Gardner Museum keeps the empty frames on the wall for visitors to see?

CHAPTER THREE: THE REAL GHOST BUSTERS

1. Do you believe in ghosts? Why or why not?

2. Why do you think people kept believing that mediums could communicate with spirits, even after the Fox sisters admitted they were making it up?

3. How do you think it would feel to have someone doubt or question an experience you had just because it can't be explained?

CHAPTER FOUR: THE CASE OF THE MISSING FEATHERS

1. Do you think Edwin's punishment was fair? Why or why not?

2. Why do you think it's important to preserve animal species in museums? What does it teach us about our world?

3. Do you think hobbies like salmon fly tying should be allowed anymore, if they inspire people to commit crimes like this?

CHAPTER FIVE: ESCAPING ALCATRAZ

1. Do you think prisons are the best way to stop people from committing crimes? Why or why not?

2. Why do you think the brothers kept trying to escape?

3. What does the word "freedom" mean to you?

4. Does this story make you think differently about what it means to be a "criminal"? Why?

CHAPTER SIX: THE SEARCH FOR AGATHA CHRISTIE

1. Why do you think Agatha never shared her secret with the world?

2. What is the impact of having your personal life shared with the public in a newspaper story? What do you think that would feel like?

CHAPTER SEVEN: SHERLOCK HOLMES AND THE FAIRY PHOTOGRAPHS

1. Do you think it was wrong for the girls to lie to Gardner and Sir Arthur Conan Doyle? Why or why not?

2. "Confirmation bias" is a kind of bias in which people look for evidence of something they already believe. How do you think confirmation bias played a role in this story?

CHAPTER EIGHT: WHO WAS D.B. COOPER?

1. Is D. B. Cooper a hero or a villain? Why do you think so?

2. Why do you think people in the Pacific Northwest still celebrate D. B. Cooper?

3. Why do you think it took Tina Mucklow multiple decades to talk about this crime? What do you think it was like for her and other crew members to survive this incident, even though no one got hurt?

CHAPTER NINE: THE PHOENIX LIGHTS

1. Do you believe in aliens? Why or why not?

2. How do you feel about the fact that the government investigated UFOs for so many years? Do you think that's a good use of our time and money, or not? Explain why.

3. Why do you think some people still believe the Phoenix Lights were caused by aliens, even though journalists have debunked that theory?

CHAPTER TEN: FOOTPRINTS IN THE SAND

1. Why do you think Al and Tony let this prank go on for so long?

2. Did it surprise you that a famous scientist told the world that the Clearwater Monster was real? Why or why not?

CHAPTER ELEVEN: SEEING LINCOLN'S GHOST

1. Do you think Mumler truly believed he could channel spirits? Or was he just trying to make money?

2. Why do you think P. T. Barnum wanted to prove Mumler wrong?

3. Was what Mumler did unethical? Explain your opinion.

CHAPTER TWELVE: THE WOMAN WITH ALL THE NUMBERS

1. Even though Stephanie St. Clair made her money illegally, many people see her as an icon and a hero. Why do you think that is?

2. Why do you think St. Clair wanted to keep white gangsters out of her neighborhood?

3. Stephanie St. Clair did a lot of good things, but she did a lot of bad things, too. What do you think about her as a character? Is she a good person? Why or why not?

CHAPTER THIRTEEN: HACKERS: HOW A FIFTEEN-YEAR-OLD SHUT DOWN NASA

1. Do you think people should go to prison for cybercrime? If so, what kinds of cybercrime, and for how long?

2. Do you think kids should go to prison for cybercrime?

3. If you were a white-hat hacker, what kinds of causes would you stand up for?

CHAPTER FOURTEEN: THE REIGN OF THE PIRATE QUEEN

1. Did hearing a story about a female pirate from China surprise? Why or why not?

2. Why do you think Ching Shih had such a strict code of conduct?

3. Why do you think the Chinese government agreed with Ching Shih's deal?

CHAPTER FIFTEEN: WHAT WE CAN LEARN FROM BONES

1. Why do you think it's important for people like Kristen to investigate deaths and find out what happened?

2. Why do you think Kristen persevered, even after she didn't get a job in her field for two years?

3. What about Kristen's story surprised you the most? Did you learn anything you didn't know before about how cases like this are solved?

NOTES

1. White, Brynn, "The Saga of Masterpiece, Part 2," American Kennel Club, July 2, 2019, https://www.akc.org/expert-advice/news/the-saga-of-masterpiece-part-2.
2. White, Brynn, "The Saga of Pulaski's Masterpiece the Poodle, Part 1," American Kennel Club, July 2, 2019, https://www.akc.org/expert-advice/news/the-saga -of-masterpiece-part-1.
3. White, "Masterpiece, Part 1."
4. White, "Masterpiece, Part 1."
5. Judge, Phoebe, "Masterpiece," *Criminal* podcast, no. 84, February 9, 2018, https:// thisiscriminal.com/episode-84-masterpiece-02-09-2018.
6. White, "Masterpiece, Part 1."
7. Judge, "Masterpiece."
8. White, "Masterpiece, Part 1."
9. Judge, "Masterpiece."
10. White, "Masterpiece, Part 1."
11. Judge, "Masterpiece."
12. White, "Masterpiece, Part 1."
13. White, "Masterpiece, Part 1."
14. White, "Masterpiece, Part 2."
15. White, "Masterpiece, Part 2."
16. Judge, "Masterpiece."
17. White, "Masterpiece, Part 2."
18. "Alexis E. Pulaski, 73, Dies; Bred and Sold Toy Poodles," *New York Times*, July 11, 1968, sec. Obituaries.
19. White, "Masterpiece, Part 2."
20. McGreevy, Nora, "Five Things to Know about the Gardner Museum Heist—The Biggest Art Theft in Modern History," *Smithsonian Magazine*, April 9, 2021, https://www.smithsonianmag.com/smart-news/five-things-know-about -isabella-stewart-gardner-art-heist-180977448.
21. Bagat, Dhruti, "Boston's Greatest Unsolved Mystery: The Gardner Museum Art Heist," Boston Public Library, April 29, 2021, https://www.bpl.org/blogs/post /bostons-greatest-unsolved-mystery-the-gardner-museum-art-heist.
22. "The Theft," Isabella Stewart Gardner Museum, accessed January 13, 2021, https://www.gardnermuseum.org/about/theft-story.
23. Siemaszko, Corky, "Here's Why Art Thieves Steal Paintings They Can't Sell," NBC News, September 30, 2016, https://www.nbcnews.com/news/world/here -s-why-art-thieves-steal-paintings-they-can-t-n657656.
24. Rea, Naomi, "Who Says Museum Heists Don't Pay? Here Are 5 Ways Crafty Criminals Actually Profit from High-Profile Art Thefts," Artnet News, August

24, 2020, https://news.artnet.com/art-world/how-thieves-profit-from-heists
-1903376.

25. Rea, "Who Says Museum Heists."

26. Rea, "Who Says Museum Heists."

27 Kurkjian, Stephen A., *Master Thieves: The Boston Gangsters Who Pulled Off the World's Greatest Art Heist*, PublicAffairs, 2015, 94.

28 McShane, Thomas, and Dary Matera, *Stolen Masterpiece Tracker: The Dangerous Life Of The FBI's #1 Art Sleuth.* Fort Lee, NJ: Barricade Books, 2006.

29. Crimaldi, Laura, "Meet the Suspects: Carmello Merlino," *Boston Herald, April 26, 2008,* https://www.bostonherald.com/2008/04/26/meet-the-suspects-carmello
-merlino.

30. Horan, Kelly, and Jack Rodolico, "Episode 4: 'Two Bad Men," Wbur.org, 2018, https://www.wbur.org/lastseen/2018/10/08/two-bad-men.

31. Kurkjian, Stephen, "Bobby Guarente," WBUR, October 12, 2018, https://www
.wbur.org/lastseen/2018/10/12/bobby-guarente.

32. Kurkjian, "Bobby Guarente."

33. Cascone, Sarah, "Robert 'Bobby' Gentile, Long Fingered by the FBI as a Suspect in the 1990 Isabella Stewart Gardner Museum Heist, Dies at 85," Artnet News, September 23, 2021, https://news.artnet.com/art-world/gardner-heist-suspect
-robert-gentile-2012506.

34. Cascone, "Robert 'Bobby' Gentile."

35. Kurkjian, "Bobby Guarente."

36. House, Dennis, "The Big Heist: Who Is Robert 'Bobby the Cook' Gentile and What Did the FBI Find at His CT Home During Their Investigation into the Biggest Art Heist in History?" WTNH, February 11, 2021, https://www.wtnh
.com/news/news-8-exclusive/the-big-heist-who-is-robert-gentile-and-what
-did-the-fbi-find-at-his-manchester-home.

37. Cascone, "Robert 'Bobby' Gentile."

38. Kurkjian, *Master Thieves*.

39. Belcher Morris, Jasmyn, "Former Security Guard Reflects on What He Lost One Fateful Night," NPR, March 13, 2015, https://www.npr.org/2015/03/13
/392567024/former-security-guard-reflects-on-what-he-lost-one-fateful
-night?t=1640654691957.

40. "A Very Brief History of the Ghost Club," The Ghost Club, accessed October 1, 2021, https://www.ghostclub.org.uk/history.html.

41. "Spiritualism." Encyclopædia Britannica, accessed October 1, 2021, https://www
.britannica.com/topic/spiritualism-religion.

42. Abbott, Karen, "The Fox Sisters and the Rap on Spiritualism," *Smithsonian Magazine,* October 30, 2012, https://www.smithsonianmag.com/history/the-fox
-sisters-and-the-rap-on-spiritualism-99663697.

43. Abbott, "The Fox Sisters."

44. "Spiritualism."

45. Abbott, "The Fox Sisters."

46. "A Very Brief History of the Ghost Club."

47. "A Very Brief History of the Ghost Club."

48. Hoskin, Peter, "Ghost Club: Yeats's and Dickens's Secret Society of Spirits," *The Paris Review*, November 1, 2017, https://www.theparisreview.org /blog/2017/10/31/ghost-club-yeats-dickens-secret-society-spirits.

49. "A Very Brief History of the Ghost Club."

50. Nash, Deborah. "At the London Ghost Club Which Meets Up in Old Pubs," Londonist, March 6, 2020, https://londonist.com/london/secret/ghost-club -london-visit-join.

51. Palmer, Alex W, "The Vanishing Mysteries of the Ghost Club," Pacific Standard, October 26, 2015, https://psmag.com/environment/meet-the-ghost-club.

52. Nash, "At the London Ghost Club."

53. Palmer, "The Vanishing Mysteries."

54. Palmer, "The Vanishing Mysteries."

55. Wallace Johnson, Kirk, "The Curious Case of the Fly-Fishing Feather Thief," *Outside*, April 19, 2018, https://www.outsideonline.com/culture/books-media /feather-thief-excerpt.

56. Wallace Johnson, "The Curious Case."

57. Cole, Sean, "The Feather Heist," podcast, *This American Life*, August 10, 2018, https://www.thisamericanlife.org/654/the-feather-heist.

58. Wallace Johnson, "The Curious Case."

59. Lidz, Franz, "The Great Feather Heist," *Smithsonian Magazine*, April 2018, https://www.smithsonianmag.com/science-nature/great-feather -heist-180968408.

60. Wallace Johnson, "The Curious Case."

61. Lidz, "The Great Feather Heist."

62. Wallace Johnson, "The Curious Case."

63. Wallace Johnson, "The Curious Case."

64. Wallace Johnson, "The Curious Case."

65. Cole, "The Feather Heist."

66. Cole, "The Feather Heist."

67. Cole, "The Feather Heist."

68. Cole, "The Feather Heist."

69. Cole, "The Feather Heist."

70. Wallace Johnson, "The Curious Case."

71. Wallace Johnson, "The Curious Case."

72. Cole, "The Feather Heist."

73. Cole, "The Feather Heist."

74. Cole, "The Feather Heist."

75. "Natural History Museum Thief Ordered to Pay Thousands," BBC, July 30, 2011, https://www.bbc.com/news/uk-england-beds-bucks-herts-14352867.

76. Cole, "The Feather Heist."

77. Cole, "The Feather Heist."

78. Cole, "The Feather Heist."

79. Cole, "The Feather Heist."

80. Cole, "The Feather Heist."

81. Cole, "The Feather Heist."

82. Lidz, "The Great Feather Heist."

83. Judge, Phoebe, "The Escape," *Criminal* podcast, no. 77, October 20, 1977, https://thisiscriminal.com/episode-77-the-escape-10-20-2017.

84. "55 Years Later, Alcatraz Prison Escape Remains a Mystery," CBS News, July 2, 2017, https://www.cbsnews.com/news/alcatraz-prison-escape-remains-a-mystery.

85. "Alcatraz Escape." 2022. *Federal Bureau Of Investigation*. Accessed January 23. https://www.fbi.gov/history/famous-cases/alcatraz-escape.

86. Judge, "The Escape."

87. Judge, "The Escape."

88. Judge, "The Escape."

89. Wallace, Jim, "Alcatraz 50 Years Later," WALB News, Jun. 11, 2002, https://www.walb.com/story/18741310/alcatraz-50-years-later.

90. Judge, "The Escape."

91. OceanView Publishing Company, "Welcome to Alcatraz History," Alcatraz History, accessed November 2, 2021, https://www.alcatrazhistory.com.

92. "San Francisco Bay, CA Ocean Water Temperature Today: UNITED STATES TEMP," SeaTemperature.info, accessed November 2, 2021, https://seatemperature.info/united-states/san-francisco-water-temperature.html.

93. OceanView Publishing Company, "Welcome to Alcatraz History."

94. "Alcatraz Escape."

95. OceanView Publishing Company, "Welcome to Alcatraz History."

96. "Alcatraz Escape."

97. Judge, "The Escape."

98. "Alcatraz Escape."

99. Wallace, "Alcatraz 50 Years Later."

100. Judge, "The Escape."

101. Judge, "The Escape."

102. Dowd, Katie, and Andrew Chamings, "Did Alcatraz's Most Famous Escapees Survive? Two SFGate Writers Disagree Completely," SFGate, October 3, 2021, https://www.sfgate.com/sfhistory/article/Did-Alcatraz-most-famous-escapees-survive-escape-15538020.php.

103. Frost, Natasha, "Was the Escape from Alcatraz Successful?" History, July 16, 2018, https://www.history.com/news/alcatraz-escape-new-evidence-anglin-brothers.

104. Judge, "The Escape."

105. Jordan, Tina, "When the World's Most Famous Mystery Writer Vanished," *New York Times,* June 11, 2019, https://www.nytimes.com/2019/06/11/books/agatha-christie-vanished-11-days-1926.html.

106. Cade, Jared, *Agatha Christie and the Eleven Missing Days*. London: Peter Owen, 2013.

107. Cade, *Agatha Christie*, 31–33.

108. Cade, *Agatha Christie*, 49.

109. Jordan, "When the World."

110. Jordan, "When the World."

111. Jordan, "When the World."

112. Jordan, "When the World."

113. Jordan, "When the World."

114. Cade, *Agatha Christie*, 91.

115. Jordan, "When the World."

116. Cade, *Agatha Christie*, 100, 102.

117. Cade, *Agatha Christie*, 108.

118. Cade, *Agatha Christie*, 107.

119. Jordan, "When the World."

120. Cade, *Agatha Christie*, 125.

121. Weinberg, Kate, "Agatha Christie's Greatest Mystery Was Left Unsolved," CrimeReads, January 30, 2020, https://crimereads.com/agatha-christies -greatest-mystery-was-left-unsolved.

122. Sonin Schlesinger, Tara, "15 Timeless Sherlock Holmes Quotes," Bookbub, January 17, 2020, https://www.bookbub.com/blog/best-sherlock-holmes -quotes.

123. Boese, Alex, "The Cottingley Fairies," The Museum Of Hoaxes, 2015, http:// hoaxes.org/photo_database/image/the_cottingley_fairies.

124. "Cottingley Fairies: How Sherlock Holmes's Creator Was Fooled By Hoax," BBC News, December 5, 2020, https://www.bbc.com/news/uk-england -leeds-55187973.

125. Boese, "The Cottingley Fairies."

126. "Cottingley Fairies: How Sherlock."

127. "Cottingley Fairies: How Sherlock."

128. "Cottingley Fairies: How Sherlock."

129. "Cottingley Fairies: How Sherlock."

130. Judge, Phoebe, "Ghost Racket Crusade," *Criminal* podcast, October 22, 2021, https://thisiscriminal.com/episode-175-ghost-racket-crusade-10-22-2021.

131. Arthur Conan Doyle, "The Most Important Thing in the World," *The Conan Doyle Estate Ltd*, accessed December 28, 2021, https://arthurconandoyle.co.uk /spiritualist.

132. Conan Doyle, "The Most Important Thing."

133. Barquin, Alexis, "Fairies Photographed," Arthur-Conan-Doyle.Com, accessed December 28, 2021, https://www.arthur-conan-doyle.com/index .php?title=Fairies_Photographed.

134. Barquin, "Fairies Photographed."

135. Losure, Mary, "Sir Arthur and the Fairies," Mental Floss, accessed December 28, 2021, https://www.mentalfloss.com/article/68395/sir-arthur-and-fairies.

136. Losure, "Sir Arthur and the Fairies."

137. Losure, "Sir Arthur and the Fairies."

138. Losure, "Sir Arthur and the Fairies."

139. Fox, Margalit, "James Randi, Magician Who Debunked Paranormal Claims, Dies at 92," *New York Times*, October 21, 2020, https://www.nytimes .com/2020/10/21/obituaries/james-randi-dead.html.

140. Boese, "The Cottingley Fairies."

141. Boese, "The Cottingley Fairies."

142. "Cottingley Fairies: How Sherlock."

143. Conan Doyle, "The Most Important Thing."

144. "D. B. Cooper Hijacking," FBI, May 18, 2016, https://www.fbi.gov/history/famous-cases/db-cooper-hijacking.

145. Marks, Andrea, "The Missing Piece of the D. B. Cooper Story," *Rolling Stone*, August 18, 2021, https://www.rollingstone.com/culture/culture-features/db-cooper-tina-mucklow-untold-story-1111944.

146. Marks, "The Missing Piece."

147. Marks, "The Missing Piece."

148. Marks, "The Missing Piece."

149. Marks, "The Missing Piece."

150. "D. B. Cooper Hijacking."

151. Marks, "The Missing Piece."

152. Marks, "The Missing Piece."

153. Marks, "The Missing Piece."

154. "D. B. Cooper Hijacking."

155. "Rackstraw: 5 Fast Facts You Need to Know," DB Cooper, June 6, 2021. https://dbcooper.com/robert-rackstraw-5-fast-facts.

156. Evans, Tim, "Here Are 11 Possible Suspects in the D. B. Cooper Mystery, Including Some Who Falsely Confessed," *Indianapolis Star*, August 3, 2018, https://www.indystar.com/story/news/2018/08/03/db-cooper-suspects-include-robert-rackstraw-false-confessions-woman/865813002.

157. Perry, Douglas, "'Charming' D. B. Cooper Suspect Sheridan Peterson Dies at 94, Spent Years Dedicated to Political Causes," *Oregon Live*, January 30, 2021, https://www.oregonlive.com/history/2021/01/charming-db-cooper-suspect-sheridan-peterson-dies-at-94-spent-years-dedicated-to-political-causes.html

158. Perry, "'Charming' D. B. Cooper Suspect."

159. "D. B. Cooper Hijacking."

160. "Richard Floyd McCoy, Jr.," FBI, May 18, 2016, https://www.fbi.gov/history/famous-cases/richard-floyd-mccoy-jr.

161. "Richard Floyd McCoy, Jr."

162. Kennedy, Lesley, "Were These Taunting Letters Really from D. B. Cooper, the Mysterious 1971 Hijacker?" History, November 2, 2020, https://www.history.com/news/db-cooper-case-fbi-letters.

163. Kennedy, "Were These Taunting Letters."

164. Kennedy, "Were These Taunting Letters."

165. Kennedy, "Were These Taunting Letters."

166. Haskins, Devon. 2021. "50 Years Later, the Quest to Solve the Mysterious D. B. Cooper Case Goes On." KGW8. https://www.kgw.com/article/news/local/db-cooper-expert-columbia-river-search/283-4a5311ba-f43f-499b-8c17-1f05eb419854.

167. Edward Helmore, "Crime Historian Digs for DB Cooper Case Evidence: 'Authorities looked in wrong area,'" *Guardian*, August 8, 2021, https://www.theguardian.com/us-news/2021/aug/08/historian-dig-db-cooper-case-evidence.

168. "D. B. Cooper Day at the Ariel General Store & Tavern," Atlas Obscura, June 21, 2013, https://www.atlasobscura.com/places/d-b-cooper-day-at-the-ariel-general-store-tavern.

169. Marks, "The Missing Piece."

170. Marks, "The Missing Piece."

171. Price, Richard, "Arizonans Say the Truth about UFO Is Out There," *USA Today*, June 18, 1997, http://www.ufosnw.com/history_of_ufo/phoenixlights1997 /usatodayarticle06181997old.pdf.

172. Price, "Arizonans Say."

173. Price, "Arizonans Say."

174. Price, "Arizonans Say."

175. Hook, John, "What Were Those Lights in the Phoenix Sky?" CNN Interactive, June 19, 1997," Wayback Machine Internet Archive, https://web.archive.org /web/20170413133442/http://edition.cnn.com/US/9706/19/ufo.lights.

176. "Roswell," History, updated June 7, 2019, https://www.history.com/topics /paranormal/roswell.

177. "Roswell."

178. "Project BLUE BOOK — Unidentified Flying Objects," US National Archives, September 29, 2020, https://www.archives.gov/research/military/air-force/ufos.

179. "Project BLUE BOOK."

180. "Roswell."

181. "Project BLUE BOOK."

182. Price, "Arizonans Say."

183. Price, "Arizonans Say."

184. Hendley, Matthew, "The 'Phoenix Lights' Are No Mystery," *Phoenix New Times*, March 14, 2014, https://www.phoenixnewtimes.com/news/the-phoenix-lights -are-no-mystery-6661825.

185. Hendley, "The 'Phoenix Lights.'"

186. Radford, Benjamin, "Mysterious Phoenix Lights a UFO Hoax," Live Science, April 23, 2008, https://www.livescience.com/2483-mysterious-phoenix-lights -ufo-hoax.html.

187. Radford, "Mysterious Phoenix Lights."

188. Radford, "Mysterious Phoenix Lights."

189. Symington, Fife, "Symington: I Saw a UFO in the Arizona Sky," CNN, November 9, 2007, http://www.cnn.com/2007/TECH/science/11/09/simington .ufocommentary/index.html.

190. Symington, "I Saw a UFO."

191. Martinez, Luis. 2021. "Pentagon Announces New Group to Investigate Reports of Ufos Near Certain Military Sites." ABC News. https://abcnews.go.com /Politics/pentagon-announces-group-investigate-reports-ufos-military-sites /story?id=81375017.

192. Rob, Lammle, "Florida's Giant Penguin," Mental Floss, October 18, 2013, https:// www.mentalfloss.com/article/52460/strange-states-floridas-giant-penguin.

193. Judge, Phoebe, "The Clearwater Monster," *Criminal* podcast, no. 152, November 13, 2020, https://thisiscriminal.com/episode-152-the-clearwater-monster.

194. Judge, "The Clearwater Monster."

195. Judge, "The Clearwater Monster."

196. Judge, "The Clearwater Monster."

197. Lammle, "Florida's Giant."

198. Klinkenberg, Jeff, and Gabrielle Calise, "Remember the Clearwater Monster? It's Having a Moment," *Tampa Bay Times,* January, 5, 2021, https://www .tampabay.com/life-culture/history/2021/01/05/remember-the-clearwater -monster-its-having-a-moment.

199. "Sanderson, Ivan T(erence) (1911–1973)." Encyclopedia.com, November 2, 2021, https://www.encyclopedia.com/science/encyclopedias-almanacs-transcripts -and-maps/sanderson-ivan-terence-1911-1973.

200. Judge, "The Clearwater Monster."

201. "Sanderson, Ivan T."

202. "Sanderson, Ivan T."

203. Judge, "The Clearwater Monster."

204. Judge, "The Clearwater Monster."

205. Hernandez, Daisy, "Prehistoric Monster Penguins: Awesome, Terrifying, or Both?," *Popular Mechanics,* November 2, 2021, https://www.popularmechanics .com/science/a28699986/giant-prehistoric-penguins.

206. "Obituary for Tony Signorini: Royal Palm North Funeral Chapel & Memorial," Royal Palm North, CFS, July 9, 2012, https://www.royalpalmnorth.com /obituary/Tony-Signorini.

207. Judge, "The Clearwater Monster."

208. Judge, "The Clearwater Monster."

209. Judge, "The Clearwater Monster."

210. Judge, "The Clearwater Monster."

211. Judge, "The Clearwater Monster."

212. Judge, "The Clearwater Monster."

213. "Obituary for Tony Signorini."

214. Judge, "The Clearwater Monster."

215. Judge, "The Clearwater Monster."

216. Judge, Phoebe, "Spiritual Developments," *Criminal* podcast, February 26, 2021, https://thisiscriminal.com/episode-159-spiritual-developments-2-26-2021.

217. Roos, Dave, "When a 19th-Century 'Spirit Photographer' Claimed to Capture Ghosts through His Lens," History, https://www.history.com/news/spirit -photography-civil-war-william-mumler.

218. Judge, "Spiritual Developments."

219. Judge, "Spiritual Developments."

220. Judge, "Spiritual Developments."

221. Judge, "Spiritual Developments."

222. Judge, "Spiritual Developments."

223. Judge, "Spiritual Developments."

224. Judge, "Spiritual Developments."

225. Roos, "When a 19th-Century."

226. Roos, "When a 19th-Century."

227. Judge, "Spiritual Developments."

228. Judge, "Spiritual Developments."

229. Judge, "Spiritual Developments."

230. "Barnum's American Museum," The Lost Museum Archive, City University of New York, accessed January 13, 2022, https://lostmuseum.cuny.edu/archive /barnums-american-museum.

231. "General Tom Thumb | Biography & Facts," 2022. *Encyclopedia Britannica*, accessed December 28, 2021. https://www.britannica.com/biography/Charles -Stratton.

232. Judge, "Spiritual Developments."

233. Judge, "Spiritual Developments."

234. Judge, "Spiritual Developments."

235. Judge, "Spiritual Developments."

236. Porath, Jason, "Stephanie St. Clair: Harlem's Queen of Numbers," Rejected Princesses, accessed December 3, 2021, https://www.rejectedprincesses.com /princesses/stephanie-st-clair.

237. Durn, Sarah, "Stephanie St. Clair, Harlem's 'Numbers Queen,' Dominated the Gambling Underground and Made Millions," *Smithsonian Magazine*, May 21, 2021, https://www.smithsonianmag.com/history/meet-stephanie-st-clair -immigrant-turned-millionaire-who-dominated-harlems-gambling -underground-180977759/.

238. Durn, "Stephanie St. Clair."

239. "The Game," *Digital Harlem Blog*, accessed December 4, 2021, https:// drstephenrobertson.com/digitalharlemblog/playing-the-numbers-the-book /learn-more-about-numbers/the-game.

240. Durn, "Stephanie St. Clair."

241. Gershon, Livia, "Madame Stephanie St. Clair: Numbers Queen of Harlem," JSTOR Daily, February 23, 2021, https://daily.jstor.org/madame-stephanie-st -clair-numbers-queen-of-harlem.

242. Durn, "Stephanie St. Clair."

243. Porath, "Stephanie St. Clair."

244. Gershon, "Madame Stephanie."

245. Gershon, "Madame Stephanie."

246. Gershon, "Madame Stephanie."

247. Harris, LaShawn, "The Queen of Numbers: Stephanie St. Clair and Harlem's Gambling Racket," The Gotham Center for New York City History, May 24, 2017, https://www.gothamcenter.org/blog/the-queen-of-numbers-stephanie-st -clair-and-harlems-gambling-racket.

248. Durn, "Stephanie St. Clair."

249. Durn, "Stephanie St. Clair."

250. Durn, "Stephanie St. Clair."

251. Durn, "Stephanie St. Clair."

252. Gershon, "Madame Stephanie."

253. Durn, "Stephanie St. Clair."

254. Stout, David, "Youth Sentenced in Government Hacking Case," *New York Times*, September 23, 2000, https://www.nytimes.com/2000/09/23/us/youth -sentenced-in-government-hacking-case.html.

255. Infosecurity, "The Life and Death Story of a Hacker Who Hacked the Pentagon and NASA at the Age of 15," *Umumble*, accessed January 13, 2022, https://

umumble.com/blogs/Infosecurity/the-life-and-death-story-of-a-hacker-who
-hacked-the-pentagon-and-nasa-at-the-age-of-15.

256. "Interviews—Anonymous," Hackers | Frontline | PBS, accessed January 13,
2022, https://www.pbs.org/wgbh/pages/frontline/shows/hackers/interviews
/anon.html.

257. Stout, "Youth Sentenced."

258. Stout, "Youth Sentenced."

259. "Interviews—Anonymous."

260. Stout, "Youth Sentenced."

261. "Interviews—Anonymous."

262. "Interviews—Anonymous."

263. "Interviews—Anonymous."

264. Kaspersky, "Black Hat, White Hat, and Gray Hat Hackers—Definition and
Explanation," AO Kaspersky Lab, accessed December 3, 2021, https://www
.kaspersky.com/resource-center/definitions/hacker-hat-types.

265. Kaspersky, "Black Hat."

266. "Interviews—Anonymous."

267. *Miami Herald*, "Jonathan Joseph James Obituary" [published May 21–22, 2008],
Legacy, https://www.legacy.com/us/obituaries/herald/name/jonathan-james
-obituary?id=23940727.

268. Stanek, Becca, "How Did Anonymous Start? The History of the Mysterious
'Hacktivist' Group Began Quite Some Time Ago," Bustle, February 20, 2015,
https://www.bustle.com/articles/65444-how-did-anonymous-start-the-history
-of-the-mysterious-hacktivist-group-began-quite-some-time-ago.

269. Stanek, "How Did Anonymous Start?"

270. Nickelsburg, Monika. 2015. "A Brief History of the Guy Fawkes Mask."
Mentalfloss.com. https://www.mentalfloss.com/article/70807/brief-history
-guy-fawkes-mask.

271. Beran, Dale, "The Return of Anonymous," *The Atlantic*, August 2020, https://
www.theatlantic.com/technology/archive/2020/08/hacker-group-anonymous
-returns/615058.

272. Sengupta, Somini, "16 Arrested as F.B.I. Hits the Hacking Group Anonymous,"
New York Times, July 20, 2011, https://www.nytimes.com/2011/07/20
/technology/16-arrested-as-fbi-hits-the-hacking-group-anonymous.html.

273. Kushner, David, "The Masked Avengers," *New Yorker*, September 8, 2014,
https://www.newyorker.com/magazine/2014/09/08/masked-avengers.

274. Kushner, "The Masked Avengers."

275. "Interviews—Anonymous."

276. Duncombe, Laura Sook, *Pirate Women: The Princesses, Prostitutes, and
Privateers Who Ruled the Seven Seas*. Chicago: Chicago Review Press, 2017.

277. Banerji, Urvija, "The Chinese Female Pirate Who Commanded 80,000
Outlaws," Atlas Obscura, April 6, 2016, https://www.atlasobscura.com/articles
/the-chinese-female-pirate-who-commanded-80000-outlaws.

278. Slappey, Kellie, "The Pirate Blackbeard," North Carolina History Project,
accessed December 3, 2021, https://northcarolinahistory.org/encyclopedia/the
-pirate-blackbeard.

279. "The Golden Age of Piracy," Royal Museums Greenwich, accessed December 3, 2021, https://www.rmg.co.uk/stories/topics/golden-age-piracy.
280. "The Golden Age of Piracy."
281. "The Golden Age of Piracy."
282. Banerji, "The Chinese Female Pirate."
283. Duncombe, *Pirate Women.*
284. Duncombe, *Pirate Women.*
285. Duncombe, *Pirate Women.*
286. Duncombe, *Pirate Women.*
287. Duncombe, *Pirate Women.*
288. Duncombe, *Pirate Women.*
289. Duncombe, *Pirate Women.*
290. Duncombe, *Pirate Women.*
291. Duncombe, *Pirate Women.*
292. Duncombe, *Pirate Women.*
293. Puchko, Kristy, "9 Female Pirates You Should Know About," Mental Floss, September 19, 2014, https://www.mentalfloss.com/article/58889/9-female-pirates-you-should-know.
294. Puchko, "9 Female Pirates."
295. Puchko, "9 Female Pirates."
296. Gramlich, John, "What the Data Says (and Doesn't Say) about Crime in the United States," Pew Research Center, November 20, 2020, https://www.pewresearch.org/fact-tank/2020/11/20/facts-about-crime-in-the-u-s.
297. Gramlich, "What the Data Says."
298. Gramlich, "What the Data Says."
299. Gramlich, "What the Data Says"
300. Gramlich, "What the Data Says."
301. Pope, Leah, "Racial Disparities in Mental Health and Criminal Justice," NAMI: National Alliance on Mental Illness," July 24, 2019, https://www.nami.org/Blogs/NAMI-Blog/July-2019/Racial-Disparities-in-Mental-Health-and-Criminal-Justice.
302. Pope, "Racial Disparities."

ACKNOWLEDGMENTS

This book wouldn't have been possible without the work of many experienced journalists, particularly Phoebe Judge and the team at *Criminal*. Thank you for the work that you do.

Thank you to my family for taking the unconventional approach and encouraging me to keep writing. Thanks also to many friends who offered pep talks and snacks when I was burning the midnight oil: Katie Centabar, Emilie Menzel, Maggie Foley, Alex Medvedeff, Lauren Handy, David Greenspan, Stevie Belchak, and many others.

And finally, a special thank you to the many students who kept me company during long, rainy afternoons at the Olympic Middle School Library. This book is for you.

ABOUT THE AUTHOR

Rebecca Valley is a writer, editor, former educator, and armchair detective from northern Vermont. She received her MFA in Poetry from UMass Amherst, where she was the winner of the 2019 Academy of American Poets Prize. She is also the former caretaker of the Olympic Middle School library, a seasoned writing teacher, and a freelance writer and curriculum designer. She has received support from the Vermont Studio Center, Bread Loaf Writer's Conference, and other organizations. She is currently working her way through the complete works of Agatha Christie. Find her online at: www.rebeccavalley.com.